ADOBE® FLASH® CS3 PROFESSIONAL
HOW-TOs
100 ESSENTIAL TECHNIQUES

MARK SCHAEFFER

Adobe® Flash® CS3 Professional How-Tos
100 Essential Techniques

Mark Schaeffer

This Adobe Press book is published by Peachpit.

Peachpit
1249 Eighth Street
Berkeley, CA 94710
510/524-2178
510/524-2221 (fax)

Find us on the Web at: www.peachpit.com
To report errors, please send a note to errata@peachpit.com

Peachpit is a division of Pearson Education

For the latest on Adobe Press books, go to www.adobepress.com
Copyright © 2008 by Mark Schaeffer

Editor: Becca Freed
Production Editor: Lisa Brazieal
Copyeditor: Kim Saccio-Kent
Proofreader: Joanne Gosnell
Compositor: ICC Macmillan Inc.
Indexer: Karin Arrigoni
Cover design: Mimi Heft
Cover and interior design: Mimi Heft

ISBN 13: 978-0-321-50898-0
ISBN 10: 0-321-50898-X

9 8 7 6 5 4 3 2 1

Printed and bound in the United States of America

Dedication

With love to Debra

Acknowledgments

The "we" that occurs so often in the following pages is not just a rhetorical substitute for "I"; a book such as this requires the efforts of many people beyond a mere author. I'd like to offer the following people my special thanks:

- My research assistants, Kyle Bashaw and Samantha Leach, who helped me write as if I know what I'm talking about.

- The editorial and production team at Peachpit Press—Becca Freed, David Morris, Eric Schumacher-Rasmussen, Kim Saccio-Kent, Joanne Gosnell, Lisa Brazieal, Karin Arrigoni, and my valued friend Karen Reichstein—whose care and expertise made this book clear, accurate, concise, and useful.

- My students and colleagues at Chabot College, particularly Gene Groppetti, Dean of Arts and Humanities, who supported my efforts and kindly looked the other way when I shirked my official duties in my effort to meet deadlines.

- My amazing wife, Debra Goldentyer, who—while managing her own busy work life—uncomplainingly assumed all my household responsibilities, kept me well supplied with fruit and cornbread, and still found time to review every chapter.

Contents

Introduction

Adobe Flash is software with multiple personalities. It's an animation program that's used not only to make small things move on computer screens, but also to create many of the full-length cartoons you see on TV. It's a multimedia authoring environment that combines text, photographs, sound, animation, and video into projects that may be artistic, entertaining, informative, or all three. It's a software development platform that allows programmers to create the powerful but easy-to-use applications that you see all over the Web. It's a friendly, intuitive program that was originally designed for anyone to use, but has evolved into a complex, professional-level tool for seasoned designers and developers.

No single book can cover all those facets thoroughly, and this book isn't even going to try. We won't describe every feature or tell you what each keystroke and menu item does; you can get that information just as easily from the Help files that come with Flash. What we *will* do is introduce you, by means of clear explanations and carefully selected examples, to 100 fundamental skills that will allow you to work productively in Flash. Once you see how Flash "thinks" and how it approaches tasks, learning to use its multiple features and options becomes much easier.

Chapters 1 through 9 constitute a complete book on their own. If you're interested in animation and multimedia, those chapters are all you'll need. If you want to move toward more interactive, user-focused projects, go on to chapters 10 and 11, which acquaint you with the versatile programming language called ActionScript.

Each chapter includes techniques of varying levels of difficulty. If you're new to Flash, you'll probably want to go through them in order. If you already have experience in Flash or related programs, feel free to skip around and pick up what you need. Scattered throughout, you'll find notes and sidebars that you may find interesting and occasionally amusing. As I tell the students in my Flash classes, "If you're not having fun, you're not doing it right."

CHAPTER ONE

Exploring the Flash Interface

If you're a first-time user of Flash, it may take you some time to get used to its sometimes quirky user interface. But even if you've used Flash before, you'll find that formerly routine tasks now have to be handled differently. In the wake of its 2006 acquisition of Macromedia (the developer of Flash and other Web-related applications), Adobe implemented a redesigned, common interface for all its products. Programs as different as Flash, Photoshop, and Premiere Pro now look similar and work in similar ways.

This first chapter will take you through launching Flash, customizing it, and preparing for a project. It's tempting to skip these steps and to dive into creating a movie, but you'll find that taking the time to configure your workspace and organize your files helps you use Flash more comfortably and efficiently.

If you're new to Flash, it's helpful to keep in mind that Flash began as an animation program for the Web. Therefore, several of its interface elements have names drawn from the world of film: A Flash file is called a *movie* (regardless of whether anything in it actually moves); the area where the visual elements of the movie are assembled is called the *Stage;* the incremental steps by which a movie's action takes place are called *frames* (like the frames on a strip of film); and long movies are sometimes divided into segments called *scenes.* Even if you plan to use Flash as a programming environment or as an interface-development tool, it's still important to see how these more advanced capabilities relate to the animation features.

#1 Starting Flash

The first time you launch Flash, you'll encounter a Software Setup screen (**Figure 1a**). In order to use the software, you have to enter your serial number no more than 30 days after installation. If the number you've entered is valid, a green check mark will appear.

When you click the Next button, you're taken to the Activation screen. Your copy of Flash won't work unless you activate it. If you are connected to the Internet, Flash will handle this automatically; if not, you have the option of activating by phone.

If you've installed Flash as part of a suite, such as Adobe Creative Suite 3 Web Standard, you may not have to activate Flash: Activating one product in the suite automatically activates all of the others.

Two's Company; Three's a Crowd

Your license agreement with Adobe permits you to install Flash on two computers—for example, one desktop and one laptop, or on one computer at home and one in the office—as long as the program isn't used simultaneously on both computers. If you want to install Flash on a third computer, you'll first have to deactivate one of the two installed copies by choosing Deactivate from the Help menu.

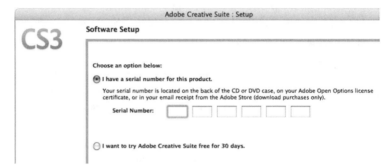

Figure 1a This setup screen appears the first time you launch Flash. If you don't have your serial number handy, you can use the program without it for up to 30 days.

Once Flash has been activated, the standard Welcome screen appears (**Figure 1b**). This screen offers shortcuts for tasks that users typically want to do when they start Flash, such as opening a previously saved file or creating various kinds of new files.

The shortcuts on the Welcome screen that you're likely to use most are in the Create New column: Flash File (ActionScript 3.0) and Flash File (ActionScript 2.0). Clicking either of these commands opens a new Flash document. If you're relatively new to Flash or to interactive scripting, ActionScript 2.0 is the preferred choice. If you have experience with object-oriented programming and you're ready to learn the latest version of the ActionScript scripting language, choose ActionScript 3.0. (For more information on the differences between ActionScript versions, see

#84.) If you plan to use Flash strictly for its animation capabilities, and you don't plan to include any interactivity in your movie, then it doesn't matter which option you select.

"Don't show again" check box   Updating billboard

Figure 1b The Welcome screen appears by default anytime you launch Flash, or anytime you have no files open in Flash.

Clicking Flash File (Mobile) launches Adobe Device Central, a program-within-a-program that simplifies creating Flash movies for handheld devices such as cell phones and personal digital assistants. Although this is a new feature in Flash CS3, it's not within the scope of this book.

The Create from Template column is useful for those who aren't yet ready to build interactive Flash movies from scratch. It offers a variety of movie templates in which the design and interactive elements are in place, so that all you have to add are the text and graphics.

What's Done Can Be Undone

If you've dismissed the Welcome screen by clicking its Close button—and you haven't selected "Don't show again"—you can bring the screen back at any time by closing all open Flash documents.

If you've clicked "Don't show again" and later you miss seeing the Welcome screen, you can bring it back by choosing Edit > Preferences (Windows) or Flash > Preferences (Mac), clicking the General category in the left column, and selecting Welcome Screen from the On Launch menu. While you're there, you may decide to let Flash display a new document or a previously open document instead.

#2 Working with Panels and Docks

The flexible workspace in Flash can be arranged in many different ways, depending on the kind of project you're working on and the environment you're comfortable with. Five basic interface elements will almost always be visible: the toolbar, the Timeline, the Stage, the panels, and the Property inspector. Although those five elements have the same functions that they did in earlier versions of Flash, their appearance and behavior have changed noticeably in Flash CS3 (**Figure 2a**).

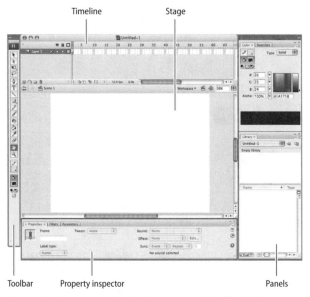

Figure 2a These are the five basic elements of the Flash CS3 user interface, shown in their default layout.

The toolbar (sometimes called the Tools panel) contains the tools you'll need to create and edit the visual elements of a Flash movie. The toolbar is now a single column, which leaves more room onscreen for the Timeline and Stage. If you prefer the two-column layout, you can toggle between single and double columns by clicking in the gray area above the toolbar.

In either layout, roll your pointer over each tool to learn the name of that tool and its keyboard shortcut. (You'll become more familiar with the contents of the toolbar when you get to Chapter 2, "Using the Drawing Tools.")

The Timeline is where you'll map out how the elements of your movie change over time. Directly below it is the Stage, where you'll create, edit, and arrange the shapes, images, video clips, and elements that make up the visual portion of your movie (**Figure 2b**).

By default, the Timeline and the Stage share a single window. You can change how much of the window the Timeline occupies by using your pointer to drag their common boundary up and down.

Timeline

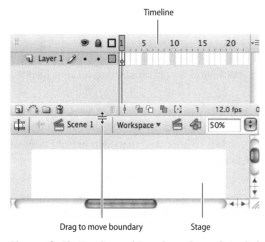

Drag to move boundary   Stage

Figure 2b The Timeline and Stage have changed very little since earlier versions of Flash.

If you wish, you can separate the Timeline from the Stage by clicking the gripper in its upper-left corner (**Figure 2c**) and dragging the Timeline away. When you do so, the Timeline becomes a dockable panel. (You'll read about docking panels on the next page.)

Gripper

Figure 2c This double column of dots represents a gripping surface that you can use to drag the Timeline away from the Stage.

The Property inspector (sometimes called the Properties panel) is located below the Stage. The Property inspector is *context-sensitive*, meaning that it displays different information depending on where you've

(continued on next page)

Panel Discussion

Flash CS3's panels represent a marriage of the best features of Adobe interfaces (such as those in Photoshop and Illustrator) with the best features of Macromedia interfaces (such as those developed for Flash and Dreamweaver). As with classic Adobe palettes, multiple panels can appear as tabbed elements in a window, and the panels can be dragged from one window to another. As with Macromedia panels, the Flash CS3 panels are dockable and collapsible. The ability to collapse an entire dock into a set of icons is brand new, however.

most recently clicked (**Figure 2d**). Whenever you need to change options or settings for tools, frames, or an entire movie, the Property inspector is where you'll usually do it.

Figure 2d The Property inspector.

Panels—the new name for what used to be called *palettes*—are where you'll find the resources you'll need for accomplishing more advanced tasks in Flash.

A group of panels is held in place by a rectangular container called a *dock*. Although Flash has only one dock by default, you can create as many additional docks as you like, all anchored to the left or right edge of the screen. A dock can be deleted, but never moved.

Within a dock, individual panels can be expanded or collapsed by clicking the light gray area above each panel (**Figure 2e**). You can also change two panels' relative sizes by dragging the boundary between them.

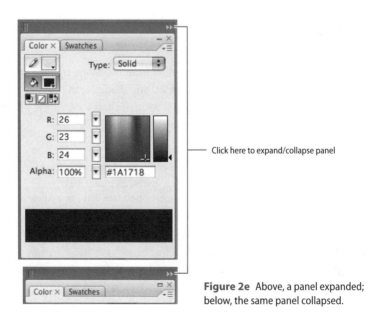

Click here to expand/collapse panel

Figure 2e Above, a panel expanded; below, the same panel collapsed.

If you need a panel that's not currently available, you can choose its name from the Window menu. If the panel was in a dock the last time it was closed, it will reappear in that dock. Otherwise, it will appear in a free-floating window. You can grab the panel by the light gray area at the top (**Figure 2f**) and drag it toward an existing dock.

Blue line

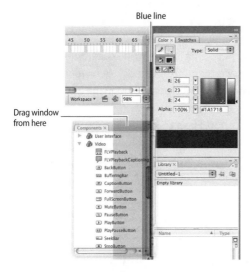

Drag window from here

Figure 2f A floating window being dragged toward a dock.

As you near the dock, a vertical blue line appears. If you drop the panel now, it will park itself in a new dock adjacent to the old one. If you continue to drag the panel onto an existing dock, a series of horizontal blue lines will appear. Each line shows where in the stack the dragged panel would land if you were to drop it immediately.

By clicking the dark gray area at the top of any dock, you can collapse all the panels in that dock to icons. Clicking an icon expands it into a panel; clicking again collapses it.

#3 Configuring Your Workspace

Any combination or arrangement of Flash windows and panels is referred to as a *workspace*. When you first launch Flash CS3, its default workspace (shown in **Figure 2a**) is rather minimal, so you're likely to want to modify it. As you work with Flash, you may find that there are certain panels you want to have available all the time, or that a certain arrangement of windows and docks feels most comfortable. If you develop a workspace that you're fond of, you can save it by choosing Window > Workspace > Save Current.

At any time, you can retrieve that saved workspace by choosing it from the Window > Workspace menu. You can delete or rename saved workspaces by choosing Window > Workspace > Manage and using the controls there.

Unlike its suitemate Photoshop, Flash CS3 doesn't come with any extra workspace presets to choose from. You'll probably want to come up with your own collection of specialized workspaces—for example, one for drawing, one for animating, and one for coding ActionScript (**Figure 3a**).

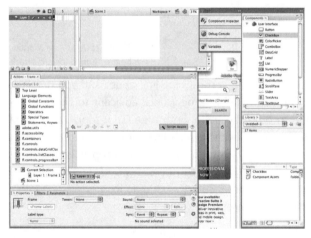

Figure 3a A sample specialized workspace for coding ActionScript. Notice that this workspace contains a much smaller Stage, and no drawing-related panels at all.

In the Mac version of Flash, the Workspace menu includes a command called Maximize Mode. When you choose this command, the title bar above the Timeline vanishes, leaving more room onscreen. The area behind the windows and panels also turns solid gray, which allows the Mac version of Flash to behave more like Flash on a Windows PC, without the desktop showing through the cracks (**Figure 3b**).

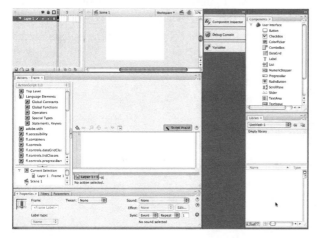

Figure 3b The workspace from Figure 3a as it looks when Maximize Mode is turned on.

#4 Setting Movie Properties

When you create a new, blank Flash movie, the first thing you'll want to do is to set the Movie Properties (also called the Document Properties)—a collection of fundamental settings that affect the entire movie.

There are two ways to set the Movie Properties: You can either choose Document from the Modify menu, thus opening the Document Properties dialog box (**Figure 4a**); or you can click on a blank area of the Stage to bring up a similar set of properties in the Property inspector. Either way, before you do anything else you'll want to set these properties: Title, Description, Dimensions, Background color, Frame rate, and Ruler units.

Food for Google

Web search engines can't see the text inside a Flash file, but they can read the file's metadata. So before you make your Flash movie available on the Web, it's a good idea to fill out the Title and Description fields in Document Properties. The information you put there allows Google and other search engines to index your movie properly and provide an accurate description in their search results.

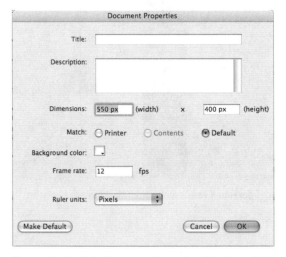

Figure 4a This is the Document Properties dialog box with its default settings.

Title and Description: These properties are examples of *metadata*, information stored in a file that gives information about that file. Filling in these fields is optional, but it's a good idea if you plan to put your Flash movie on the Web.

Dimensions: This property determines the height and width of the Stage. Since most Flash movies are designed to be viewed onscreen, it's common practice to specify movie dimensions in pixels rather than in inches or points.

The default dimensions of 550 by 400 pixels are arbitrary. Make your movie's dimensions as large or as small as you think appropriate. The only time you'll need to pay special attention to the dimensions is when you're using Flash to produce animation for video. In that case, the video editing program will specify what the dimensions of the movie should be—typically 720 by 486 pixels.

There are two shortcuts, represented by the radio buttons to the right of the label Match. (The third button resets the default dimensions.) Printer sets the movie's dimensions to match the printable area of your currently selected printer, and Contents makes the movie's dimensions match the dimensions of whatever's on the Stage. Think carefully before you make your selection. Although it's simple to change the dimensions later, it's much more difficult to modify your movie to fit the new settings.

Background color: This property determines what color the Stage will be. Whatever color you choose will show through on all unoccupied areas of the Stage. For information on picking a color, see #9.

Frame rate: The significance of the frame rate is explained in #31. Frame rate is a measure of how fast your movie progresses. For now, it's enough to know that 12 to 15 frames per second (fps) is typical for Flash movies that are posted on the Web, and that 30 fps (or, more precisely, 29.97 fps) is the standard for animation created for video use.

Ruler units: This property doesn't affect the movie, but only affects how the movie and its contents are measured in Flash. If you've specified the movie's dimensions in pixels, it's usually good to set ruler units to pixels as well.

If you want to make these new Document Properties the default settings for future movies, click the Make Default button at the lower-left corner of the dialog box. Note that the text you enter for Title and Description are not saved with the default settings; you have to enter new metadata for each new movie you create.

#5 Using Function Keys and Keyboard Shortcuts

Because creating a Flash movie can be time-consuming, it's helpful to find ways to speed up the process. One of the best ways is to master the built-in keyboard shortcuts that let you execute Flash commands with a single keystroke instead of having to choose each one from a menu.

The most common Flash tasks can be accomplished by use of function keys (those keys at the top of your keyboard labeled F1, F2, and so on). There are several function keys—F5, F6, and F7, for example—that are vital for creating animation and therefore should become a part of your vocabulary. (The specific uses of these keys are explained in Chapter 4, "Creating Animation.")

Using the function keys in Flash is often a problem for Mac users. Mac OS X reserves some function keys for its own use, and those keys don't work properly in Flash. The most commonly affected keys are F9 through F12, which the operating system uses to control Apple features such as Dashboard and Exposé. This is especially frustrating in the case of the F9 key, which in Flash is used to open some commonly used panels.

There are two ways to get around this problem. The first is to go into Mac OS X System Preferences and remap the Dashboard and Exposé features to a different set of keystrokes. The second is to go into Flash and remap its F9 through F12 features. Since this is a book about Flash, we'll look at the second alternative.

Second Helpings

When you choose Help > Flash Help, a Help panel opens inside Flash. Unlike the Help window in earlier versions, this is a dockable and collapsible panel that can be integrated with the other panels.

For added flexibility, Adobe has adopted an idea that was pioneered by Macromedia: not just having help files on the local computer, but also making the complete Help system available on the Web. On computers that are connected to the Internet, this Web-based Help system (originally called LiveDocs) acts as a natural extension of the local Help system installed with the program.

Each page in the Help panel has a link at the bottom labeled "View comments on LiveDocs" or "This page on the Web." Clicking that link opens the corresponding page in your Web browser. Unlike the Help files installed on your computer, the ones on the Web are continually revised and updated. In addition, the Web pages offer help by Adobe staff and advice from other Flash users.

To remap keyboard shortcuts in Flash:

1. Choose Edit > Keyboard Shortcuts (Windows) or Flash > Keyboard Shortcuts (Mac). You'll see the Keyboard Shortcuts dialog box (**Figure 5a**).

"Duplicate Set" button

Figure 5a The Keyboard Shortcuts dialog box.

The "Current set" menu should be set to Adobe Standard copy, which is the default set of keyboard shortcuts for Flash CS3.

2. To the right of the "Current set" menu, there is a row of four buttons. Click the first button, Duplicate Set. (The original Adobe Standard set can't be modified.)

You'll see a Duplicate dialog box, with a default name ("Adobe Standard copy") filled in.

3. Either accept the default name by clicking OK, or type a new one and click OK.

The "Current set" menu now displays the name of your duplicate set.

4. If you know the name of the command whose keyboard shortcut you want to modify, locate it by choosing the appropriate list of commands

(continued on next page)

from the Commands menu, then make your selection from one of the submenus (**Figure 5b**).

Figure 5b The submenus in the Commands menu correspond to the Flash menus on which those commands appear.

If you want to know which command a particular key combination is assigned to, you'll have to search through every submenu within the command lists. You're looking for a particular keystroke (for example, Shift-F9, which opens the Color panel).

5. Highlight the desired command.

The Description field defines the command, while the Shortcuts field shows the currently applied keystroke. The same keystroke appears in the "Press key" field.

6. Highlight the keystroke in the "Press key" field, then press the key (or key combination) that you want to replace it with.

If a "This keystroke is already assigned" error message appears, keep trying key combinations until you find one that's open.

7. Click OK.

The Keyboard Shortcuts dialog box closes, and the new keyboard shortcut takes effect.

If you just want to learn the existing keyboard shortcuts, look in the standard Flash menus. For each command that has a keyboard shortcut, the keystroke appears to the right of the command.

#6 Organizing Your Files

Flash is capable of saving and exporting a number of different file types, including QuickTime movie files, animated GIF files, projector files, and more. No matter what sort of work you're doing in Flash, there are two types of files you'll use: FLA, usually pronounced *flah*, and SWF, usually pronounced *swiff* (**Figure 6a**).

Figure 6a FLA files and SWF files can be recognized by their icons. The icon for a FLA file is on the left; that for a SWF file is on the right.

FLA is a proprietary Flash authoring file format. A FLA file contains all the information Flash needs to create and modify your movie: vector shapes, symbols, uncompressed images and sounds, Timeline information, text, uncompiled ActionScript code, and so on. For this reason, FLA files tend to be large, sometimes in the hundreds of megabytes.

To generate a FLA file, you open or create a movie in Flash and then choose File > Save (or File > Save As). The only way to view or edit a FLA file is to open it in Flash.

SWF is the Flash Player file format. A SWF file contains only the essential data needed to display your movie, and the remaining information is highly compressed. A FLA file of many megabytes may yield a SWF file of only a few kilobytes. Although the size of the FLA file doesn't matter (as long as it fits on your hard drive!), your goal in creating a Flash movie should always be to end up with as small a SWF file as possible. You'll learn some tricks for decreasing the size of SWF files in Chapter 2, "Using the Drawing Tools."

You generate a SWF file by opening a FLA file in Flash and either testing (see #35) or publishing the movie (see #79). To modify a SWF file, you'll have to open its corresponding FLA file in Flash, make your changes, and generate a new SWF file to replace the old one. With some minor exceptions, SWF files can't be edited; they can only be played.

SWF is an open format: Although it originated with Flash, many programs other than Flash can create SWF files, and some non-Adobe programs can play them, such as Apple's QuickTime player.

(continued on next page)

If you plan to include Flash movies on a Web site, you'd upload SWF files. FLA files are strictly for your own use (**Figure 6b**).

SWF file playing in browser

Figure 6b When a Flash movie appears on a Web page, what you're seeing is a SWF file, not a FLA.

As with all computer work, you should save your FLA files frequently while you're working on them. Instead of choosing File > Save each time you save your FLA file, it's a much better idea to choose File > Save As and give each new version of the file an incremental name (for example, mymovie01.fla, mymovie02.fla, and so on). You'll avoid overwriting earlier versions of your files, and you'll have a variety of different stages that you can return to if you wish.

CHAPTER TWO

Using the Drawing Tools

Before the introduction of Flash, most popular graphics programs were designed to create and edit bitmapped graphics. A bitmapped graphic (also known as a *raster graphic* or simply a *bitmap*) is made up of small squares called *pixels*.

Flash was one of the first popular programs to rely primarily on vector graphics instead of bitmaps. Vector graphics are essentially mathematical formulas that tell the computer what to draw. One of the innovations in Flash was a new set of tools that made creating vector graphics as simple and intuitive as creating bitmapped graphics.

Since then, other programs such as Adobe Illustrator have also simplified the process of making vector graphics, but the implementation of vector drawing in Flash is different from that in other programs. To work in Flash, you need to be familiar with the idiosyncratic way that Flash handles vector graphics.

#7 Getting Familiar with Paths

The most basic element of a vector drawing is a *path*, a series of anchor points connected by either straight lines or curves. Think of the anchor points as a skeleton that gives a path its structure, and think of the connecting lines or curves as skin stretched over the skeleton.

Paths can be open or closed. An open path has a beginning and end, marked by anchor points known as *endpoints*. A closed path completely encloses an area; it has no beginning and no end (**Figure 7a**). You create paths using drawing tools such as the Pen, the Pencil, and the Brush, all of which you'll learn about later in this chapter.

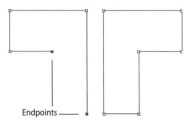

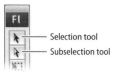

Endpoints

Figure 7a On the left is an open path; on the right is a closed path. Anchor points are represented in Flash by small squares.

To do anything to an existing path—such as edit, move, or delete it— you must tell Flash which path or paths you want to work with by selecting it with a tool. The two most important such tools are the Selection tool (the black arrow), and the Subselection tool (the white arrow) (**Figure 7b**).

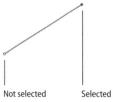

Selection tool
Subselection tool

Figure 7b The Selection and Subselection tools are probably the most frequently used items on the Flash toolbar.

To use these tools, click the item you wish to select. The fundamental difference between them is that the Selection tool is used to select an entire path, while the Subselection tool is used for individual anchor points within a path. A selected anchor point is represented by a filled-in circle; an unselected anchor point is represented by a hollow circle (**Figure 7c**).

Not selected   Selected

Figure 7c When you use the Subselection tool to select one or more anchor points in a path, all the anchor points in the path—whether selected or not—become visible.

One of the innovations in Flash was allowing a user to work with vector paths without always having to pay attention to anchor points. For example, if you wanted to change a straight line into a curve in a traditional vector drawing program, you'd have to select the anchor points at each end of the curve and manipulate them. (You can still do this in Flash if you want to; you'll see how when we look at the Pen tool in #14.) In Flash, however, you can turn a line into a curve simply by dragging a portion of the line outward with the Selection tool.

To do this, position the pointer anywhere between two anchor points. A small curve appears next to the pointer, alerting you that dragging from this point will reshape the line or curve (**Figure 7d**).

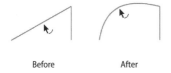

Before   After

Figure 7d When you see a small curve next to the black arrow, it means that you're in position to reshape a line or curve.

If you position the Selection tool over an anchor point, a small right angle appears next to the pointer (**Figure 7e**). This alerts you that dragging from this location will change the position of the anchor point itself, rather than reshaping the line or curve that connects two anchor points.

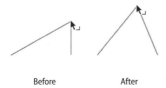

Before   After

Figure 7e When you see a small right angle next to the black arrow, it means that you're in position to move an individual anchor point.

To use either of these techniques, make sure the path that you want to edit isn't currently selected. (To deselect a selected path, click somewhere outside it with the Selection tool.)

#8 Working with Strokes and Fills

Strictly speaking, a path is a mathematical abstraction: Anchor points have no size, and the lines or curves that connect them have no thickness. To make a path visible, we have to give it a stroke, a fill, or both.

A *stroke* is an outline; a *fill* is what occupies the space enclosed by the stroke. A stroke has both weight (thickness) and color; a fill has only color (**Figure 8a**).

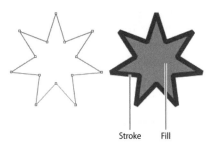

Stroke   Fill

Figure 8a A plain path is on the left; on the right, the same path has a stroke and fill added.

Drawing tools handle strokes and fills in different ways; for example, the Pencil and Line tools create only strokes, and the Brush tool creates only fills. Most drawing tools are designed to create a stroke and a fill simultaneously, however.

Even when a stroke and a fill are created at the same time with the same tool, Flash considers the stroke and the fill to be separate objects that can be selected and edited individually. To indicate that a stroke or fill has been selected, Flash covers it with a dot screen (**Figure 8b**).

Stroke selected   Fill selected   Both selected

Figure 8b The selection dot screen appears black when it's superimposed over a light-colored stroke or fill, but appears white when it's superimposed on a dark-colored stroke or fill.

The Selection tool is used with various Flash-specific mouse-click combinations that let you select some or all of a stroke and/or fill:

- To select the portion of a stroke between the two nearest anchor points, single-click the portion of the stroke you want to select.

- To select an entire stroke, double-click anywhere on the stroke.

- To select a fill, single-click the fill.

- To select a path's entire stroke *and* fill, double-click the fill.

- If a path has a stroke and you want to add a fill, click the Paint Bucket tool on the toolbar, then click anywhere in the area enclosed by the stroke.

- If a path has a fill and you want to add a stroke, click the Ink Bottle tool on the toolbar, then click the fill.

Another interface feature that's unique to Flash is the way strokes and fills interact with each other. When you select a path, move it so it overlaps another path, and then deselect it, the following things happen:

- If two stroked paths overlap each other, a new anchor point forms at each place where the strokes intersect.

- If two filled paths overlap each other, the fills are the same color, and the top path has no stroke, the two paths merge into a single path.

- If two filled paths overlap each other and the top fill has a stroke, the top path deletes the portion of the bottom path that's directly beneath it. This occurs regardless of the fill colors.

- If two filled paths overlap each other and the fills are different colors, the top path deletes the portion of the bottom path that's directly beneath it. This occurs regardless of whether the top fill has a stroke.

(continued on next page)

Seeing All the Options

Despite the standardization of interfaces across Adobe's product line, one Flash oddity has remained: a context-sensitive zone at the bottom of the toolbar known as the *options area*. When you select a tool in the toolbar, you generally need to set the tool's properties to make it suitable for the task at hand. Most of those settings can be made in the Property inspector, but some are made by means of menus and icons that appear in the options area. The location of a particular control isn't always predictable—for example, the thickness of a pencil stroke is set in the Property inspector, but the thickness of a brushstroke is set in the options area—so it's always a good idea to look in both places.

Once you get used to them, these interactions can be useful. For example, the ability of one fill to erase a differently colored fill beneath it makes it easy to cut a hole in a filled path, something that's more difficult in a traditional vector drawing program such as Illustrator (**Figure 8c**).

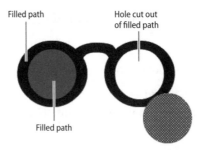

Filled path

Hole cut out of filled path

Filled path

Figure 8c On the left, two fills of different colors overlap each other. On the right, the top fill is moved away, revealing the eaten-away area underneath.

There may be times, however, when you don't want strokes or fills to interact in these ways. You can prevent these interactions by doing one of the following:

- Group each stroked or filled path individually before placing it on top of the other. (Grouping, a way of making several objects selectable as a single item, is covered in #17.) Although a group is designed to contain multiple objects, it's perfectly okay for it to contain just one.

- Place each stroked or filled path on a separate layer. (Layers are covered in #21.)

- Before creating each path, click the Object Drawing icon in the options area of the toolbar (**Figure 8d**). Doing so causes the drawing tool to create a special type of path called a Drawing Object. Like the paths found in traditional vector programs, a Drawing Object has a stroke and fill that are inseparable.

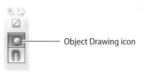

Object Drawing icon

Figure 8d When a drawing tool is selected, this icon appears in the options area at the bottom of the toolbar. Selecting it causes the drawing tool to create a Drawing Object rather than a standard path.

#9 Choosing Colors

A stroke or fill must have a color. To choose the color for a stroke, click the Stroke Color control on the toolbar. To choose the color for a fill, click the Fill Color control (**Figure 9a**).

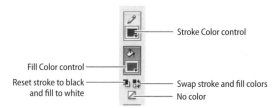

Stroke Color control

Fill Color control

Reset stroke to black and fill to white

Swap stroke and fill colors

No color

Figure 9a The Stroke Color and Fill Color controls are in the bottom third of the toolbar. (An identical set of controls is in the upper-left corner of the Color panel.)

When you click the small rectangle on either color control, a pop-up window appears (**Figure 9b**). Within it, you can choose a color either by clicking a color swatch, or by replacing the contents of the Hex Edit box with a hexadecimal color number, or by clicking the System Color Picker icon, to bring up a color-selection window.

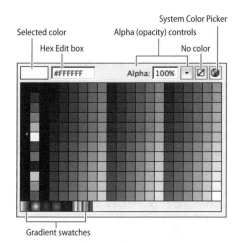

Selected color

Hex Edit box

System Color Picker

Alpha (opacity) controls

No color

Gradient swatches

Figure 9b The pop-up window for selecting colors. (The "No color" icon doesn't create a colorless stroke or fill; rather it causes Flash to omit the stroke or fill entirely.)

Once you've selected a stroke or fill color, it will be applied to all subsequent paths you create until you choose another color. If any paths are selected when you choose a stroke or fill color, the new color is applied to them as well.

(continued on next page)

That's Nice, but Do You Have It in Peach?

To change the color of an existing stroke or fill, select the element, then choose a new color via the toolbar or Color panel.

To change one color to another throughout your movie, you can use the little-known Find and Replace Color feature. Choose Edit > Find and Replace; then set the For menu to Color. Specify the current color and its replacement by choosing them from pop-up windows. You can now find and replace colors the same way you'd find and replace text.

Another way to choose stroke and fill colors is to use the Color panel (**Figure 9c**). (If it's not part of your workspace, choose Window > Color.) The upper-left corner of the Color panel has color controls identical to those on the toolbar, but the panel also offers two color-selection tools not found elsewhere.

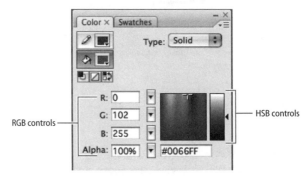

Figure 9c The Color panel allows you to specify colors by either of two systems: RGB and HSB. You can use the RGB controls either by typing a value into one of the fields, or by clicking the black triangle next to the field to access a slider.

The first tool is a set of RGB sliders for mixing varying amounts of red, green, and blue to get the color you want. (Red, green, and blue can be combined to form any color your computer is capable of displaying.)

The second tool is a set of hue, saturation, and brightness (HSB) controls. Choose a hue and saturation by clicking anywhere in the multicolored square. (Moving horizontally across the square changes the hue; moving up and down increases and decreases the saturation.) Choose a brightness for the selected color by clicking anywhere in the vertical rectangle to the right of the square.

A final way to choose colors is to use the Eyedropper tool. When you select the Eyedropper in the toolbar and click a stroke, the Stroke Color controls in the toolbar and Color Palette display the color of the stroke you clicked. When you click a fill, the Fill Color controls change similarly.

#10 Creating Gradients

A gradient is a series of colors that blend smoothly into one another. They're often used to give flat objects the illusion of depth (**Figure 10a**).

To create a gradient, you need a starting color and a destination color. If you wish, you can add one or more intermediate colors.

Flash supports two kinds of gradient: linear and radial. A linear gradient proceeds in a straight line from the starting color to the destination color; a radial gradient proceeds outward in a circular pattern, with the starting color at the center of the circle and the destination color at the edge.

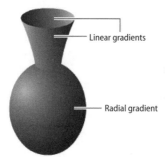

Linear gradients

Radial gradient

Figure 10a This simple vase has two kinds of gradient fills.

The simplest way to create a gradient stroke or fill is to choose one of the gradient swatches from a pop-up window in the Stroke Color or Fill Color control. (See **Figure 9b** in #9.)

In most cases, the simple black-and-white or primary-colored gradient that you choose from the window won't suit your needs. You'll want to

(continued on next page)

modify the colors, or perhaps add some intermediates. You use the Color panel (**Figure 10b**) to do either.

If a gradient fill or stroke is currently selected, or the Fill Color or Stroke Color control is set to a gradient, the Color panel displays that gradient. Otherwise, you can create a new gradient in the Color panel by choosing Linear or Radial from the Type menu.

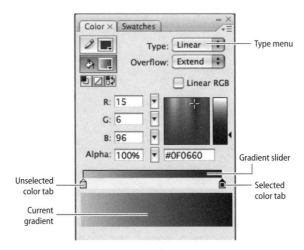

Figure 10b When Linear or Radial is selected on the Type menu, the Color panel displays these controls.

Initially, the gradient slider has two color tabs, one at each end, representing the starting and destination colors. By default, the starting color is black and the destination color is white. To change either of those colors, click the square part of the appropriate color tab and use any of the controls on the Color panel to choose a color. Alternatively, you can double-click the color tab and choose a swatch from the pop-up menu.

To add a new color to a gradient, click the point in the gradient slider at which you want the new color to appear; an additional color tab will appear at that position. To delete a color from a gradient, drag its color tab away from the gradient slider. To change the position of any color, drag its color tab to the appropriate point along the gradient slider.

In many cases, you'll not only want to customize your gradient; you'll also want to change how the gradient is applied to a selected path. If so, choose the Gradient Transform tool from the toolbar and click the stroke or fill that you want to change. (If the Gradient Transform tool isn't visible in the toolbar, hold down your mouse button over the Free Transform tool and choose Gradient Transform tool from the menu that appears.)

When you click a stroke or path with the Gradient Transform tool, a set of controls appears around the gradient. For linear gradients, the controls allow you to change the extent and direction of the gradient; for radial gradients, the controls also allow you to change the shape and the center point of the gradient (**Figure 10c**).

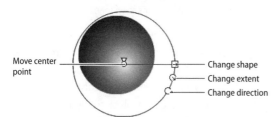

Move center point · · · · · · · · · · · Change shape
· · · · · · · · · · · Change extent
· · · · · · · · · · · Change direction

Figure 10c When a radial gradient is selected with the Gradient Transform tool, these controls become available. You can drag the controls to change different characteristics of the gradient.

#11 Setting Options for Drawing Tools

Option controls appear in the options area of the toolbar (the lower portion) and in the Property inspector (**Figure 11a**). If a tool is selected in the toolbar, these controls affect how the tool operates; if an existing path is selected, these controls change the characteristics of that path.

Aside from the Stroke Color and Fill Color controls, these are the option controls you're most likely to use regularly:

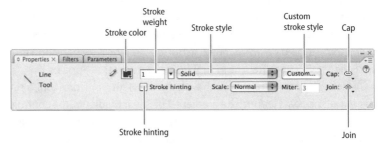

Figure 11a This set of option controls appears in the Property inspector when the Line tool is selected in the toolbar. Using other drawing tools, or selecting existing fills or strokes, will cause the options to change.

- **Stroke weight.** To adjust the lightness or heaviness of a stroke, use the Stroke Weight controls in the Property inspector. You can type a number directly into the field, or you can choose a weight interactively using the slider. (To access the slider, click the black triangle just to the right of the Stroke Weight field.) Note that Flash isn't consistent in its terminology; stroke weight is also called *height* or *thickness*.

- **Stroke style.** A stroke can appear solid, dotted, or dashed; it can have a hand-drawn or painted look; it can be straight or wavy. To make basic adjustments to the style of a stroke, use the "Stroke style" menu in the Property inspector. To make more elaborate changes, click the Custom button to the right of the slider. A dialog box appears in which you can adjust the type, pattern, wave height, and wave length of a stroke. You can adjust the stroke weight—here called thickness—in the same dialog box.

- **Stroke caps and joins.** The Cap and Join menus are to the right of the Custom button icon in the Property inspector. The Cap menu lets you decide whether the ends of a stroke will be rounded, squared off, or unmodified. The Join menu applies to the points where two segments of a stroke meet: You can decide whether the corners will be mitered, rounded, or beveled (**Figure 11b**).

Mitered   Rounded   Beveled

Figure 11b These three paths show the difference between a mitered corner, a rounded corner, and a beveled corner.

- **Stroke hinting.** Although the objects that you create with the drawing tools are vector objects, they are displayed as bitmaps. In some cases, a stroke may fall into gaps between pixels, making it appear faint or blurry on the screen. Selecting the "Stroke hinting" check box in the Property inspector prevents this from happening.

- **Smoothing.** This set of controls (a text field and a slider) appears for the tools that require freehand drawing, the Pencil and the Brush. Drawing smooth lines and curves is difficult with a graphics tablet, but it's almost impossible with a mouse or trackball. Smoothing automatically makes a rough hand-drawn path more regular and gentle. The degree of smoothing can be set anywhere from 0 (no smoothing) to 100. Note that with the Brush tool, a high setting may distort the shape of the brushstroke, making it appear uneven.

- **Snap to objects.** This option is represented by a horseshoe magnet icon in the options area of the toolbar. If the icon is selected, it makes a path "magnetic," meaning that the path will try to line up with other objects when you drag and drop it. Other kinds of snapping (to a grid, for example) can be selected from the menu at View > Snapping.

#12 Using the Primitive Shape Tools

Flash offers a variety of shape tools such as ellipses and polygons. In most other programs, these simple shapes are called primitives, but Adobe reserves the term *primitive objects* for a feature new in Flash CS3: shapes with characteristics that can be changed dynamically by controls in the Property inspector.

Both the standard and primitive shape tools are listed in a single menu in the toolbar, which you can see by holding down your mouse button over the Rectangle tool. The standard shape tools available are the Rectangle, Oval, and Polystar, which can be used to create either polygons or stars. The primitive shape tools are Rectangle Primitive and Oval Primitive; there is as yet no Polystar Primitive tool.

To see the difference between these two types of tools, let's look at the procedure for drawing a rectangle with rounded corners:

1. Select either the Rectangle or the Rectangle Primitive tool in the toolbar. A set of option controls appears in the Property inspector (**Figure 12a**).

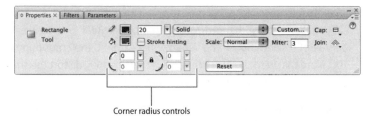

Corner radius controls

Figure 12a These controls appear in the Property inspector for both the Rectangle tool and the Rectangle Primitive tool.

2. Set a corner radius value, either by typing it into the appropriate field in the Property inspector or by using the adjacent slider. The higher the number, the more round the rectangle's corners will be. The default is

for all the corners to be equally round, in which case you enter one value. If you want the corners to have different degrees of roundness, click the Lock icon and then enter a value in each of the four fields.

3. Click and drag the mouse to draw the rectangle on the Stage. The corners are automatically rounded to the degree you specified.

These steps are the same, regardless of whether you use the Rectangle or the Rectangle Primitive tool; but the resulting rectangles have several significant differences:

- **Editability.** Let's say you don't like the setting you used for the corners—you want them to be more rounded. If you drew the rectangle with the Rectangle tool, you can't change the roundness of the corners; you have to delete the rectangle and draw it again with a new corner radius value. If you drew the rectangle with the Rectangle Primitive tool, you can simply enter a new value in the Property inspector and see the corners change instantly.

- **Flexibility.** Let's say you want to reshape the rectangle in some way, such as turning the straight sides into curves or cutting a hole in the middle of the fill. If you drew the rectangle with the Rectangle tool, you can do these kinds of things easily. If you drew the rectangle with the Rectangle Primitive tool, you can't. The *only* characteristics of a primitive object that can be changed are those that are controlled from the Property inspector, such as the object's width, height, and location on the Stage.

- **Convertibility.** You can convert a primitive object to a drawing object by double-clicking it with the Selection tool and then choosing OK. The reverse is not true: You can't convert any type of object into a primitive object.

(continued on next page)

Turning the Corner

When you create a rectangle with rounded corners, the maximum corner radius value that you can use is one-half the shortest dimension of the rectangle. For example, if the rectangle is 75 pixels wide and 50 pixels high, the corner radius value must be 25 or less. You can enter larger values, but they won't have any effect.

To create a rectangle with standard sharp corners, use 0 for the corner radius value.

For an attractive cut-out corner effect, try using a negative number for the corner radius value.

The Oval Primitive tool works like the Rectangle Primitive tool, except that it allows different characteristics to be set: The "Start angle" and "End angle" values allow you to create pie-shaped wedges (or pies with wedges cut out of them); and the "Inner radius" setting allows you to create donut-shaped objects (**Figure 12b**).

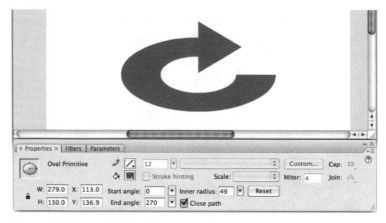

Figure 12b The curved shaft of this arrow is an oval primitive object, with settings as shown on the Property inspector. The arrowhead is a three-sided polygon made with the Polystar tool.

Tip

To create a perfect square, hold down the Shift key while drawing a rect-angle with the Rectangle tool or the Rectangle Primitive tool. Similarly, to create a perfect circle, hold down the Shift key while drawing an ellipse with the Oval tool or the Oval Primitive tool.

The shape tools, whether standard or primitive, can be handy for making things other than geometric shapes. In many cases, you'll find that the easiest way to draw something is to start with a simple shape and modify it. For example, the vase in **Figure 10a** (see #10) is constructed from two ellipses and a modified rectangle.

#**13** Using the Pencil Tool

If you're accustomed to drawing with pen or pencil on paper, you'll find the Pencil tool to be intuitive. Simply select it in the toolbar and draw with your mouse (or other input device). Depressing the mouse button creates a new path; releasing the mouse button ends the path.

The line you've created is a standard vector path with a stroke applied. You can modify it in the same ways you'd modify any other path—for example, by changing the stroke's weight or color, or by dragging anchor points with the Subselection tool.

When you select the Pencil tool in the toolbar, a Pencil Mode menu appears in the options area (**Figure 13a**). The menu gives you three choices:

Figure 13a This menu appears in the options area of the toolbar when the Pencil tool is selected.

- **Straighten.** Select this option to convert a curved line into a series of straight line segments. It also activates a shape-recognition feature that allows you to draw smooth geometric shapes. For example, if you use the Pencil tool to draw a path that's approximately oval-shaped, Flash will convert the path automatically to a perfect oval.

- **Smooth.** This setting leaves your path fundamentally as you drew it, but makes it smoother and more elegant. This is the option most people prefer: Instead of displaying the path you actually drew, it gives you the path you *wanted* to draw. The Smoothness control in the Property inspector (see #11) is available only when this option is selected.

(continued on next page)

A Hole in the Bucket

Because the Pencil tool is imprecise, drawing a closed path is sometimes difficult. You may *think* you've closed the path, but there could be a gap between the starting and ending anchor points that's too small to notice.

This gap becomes a problem only if you decide to fill the path. Because the Paint Bucket's default behavior is to fill only closed paths, you may click repeatedly inside your path without being able to fill it.

You could zoom in very closely on the suspected gap and try to close it with the Pencil tool. An easier way is to use the Gap Size menu, which appears in the options area of the toolbar whenever the Paint Bucket tool is selected.

The Gap Size menu determines how big a gap the Paint Bucket will overlook. You'll almost always want to choose Close Large Gaps; what Flash calls a "large gap" is what most of us would consider to be very small. When you make this choice, the more-tolerant Paint Bucket is likely to fill the path.

- **Ink.** If you want the path to appear exactly the way you drew it, use this option. Since most input devices (with the possible exception of a stylus and pressure-sensitive tablet) are ill-suited for drawing, you're not likely to use this setting very often (**Figure 13b**).

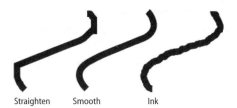

Straighten   Smooth   Ink

Figure 13b The same path has been drawn with three different options.

The Pencil tool creates strokes without fills. (The Fill Color control has no effect when the Pencil tool is selected.) If you create a closed path with the Pencil tool and then want to fill it, you can select the Paint Bucket tool and click in the enclosed area of the path.

Note
The Brush tool is similar to the Pencil tool, except that the "brushstrokes" it creates are fills rather than strokes. To add a stroke to a path created by the Brush tool, select the Ink Bottle tool and click the path.

#**14** Using the Pen Tool

The Pen may be the most unintuitive tool you'll ever encounter. If you're willing to master it, however, you'll come to appreciate the degree of control that it provides. No other drawing tool can create lines and curves as precisely.

Note
The Pen tool has been upgraded and standardized in Flash CS3. It now works like the Pen tools in Illustrator and Photoshop.

To draw with the Pen tool, there's one basic rule you must remember: *You can't draw with the Pen tool.* More specifically, you can't use it in the way you'd expect, by dragging your mouse around the Stage.

The Pen tool simply lets you create anchor points. As you create each new anchor point, Flash automatically connects it to the previous one with a line or curve. You can create three kinds of anchor points with this tool (**Figure 14a**):

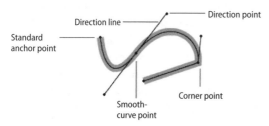

Figure 14a This path contains anchor points of all three types.

- **Anchor point.** To create an anchor point with the Pen tool, place the mouse pointer where you want the anchor point to be, and click—that is, press and release the mouse button. If you then create another anchor point (by moving the pointer and clicking again), Flash connects it to the previous one with a straight line. By making several anchor points sequentially, you can create a path consisting of a series of line segments. (We'll refer to this type as a *standard anchor point* when necessary to distinguish it from the other two types.)

(continued on next page)

Tip
To end a path, click the Pen tool icon in the toolbar after creating the last anchor point. When you make a new anchor point, Flash won't connect it to the previous one.

- **Smooth-curve point.** To create this kind of anchor point, press the mouse button, but don't release it—instead, drag it outward. As you do so, you'll see a pair of thin lines, called *direction lines,* extend outward from the anchor point. These direction lines distinguish a smooth-curve point from a standard anchor point. Each direction line is capped with a diamond-shaped handle called a *direction point.* When you create a second smooth-curve point, Flash automatically connects it to the previous one with a curve. Read on to learn how to use direction points to control the shape and size of the curve.

- **Corner point.** A corner point is the place where two curves—or a line and a curve—meet. It's essentially two anchor points in one; that is, it presents one face to the anchor point before it and another to the anchor point after it. A corner point may be half standard anchor point and half smooth-curve anchor point, or it may be a hybrid of two smooth-curve anchor points. You can recognize a corner point easily because it has only one direction line, or because it has two direction lines that point in different directions.

  You can make a corner point by modifying a smooth-curve point. To do so, choose the Subselection tool from the toolbar. Then, while holding down the Alt key (Windows) or Option key (Mac), drag either of the two direction points that are attached to an existing smooth-curve point. In doing so, you convert the smooth-curve point (with two direction lines moving in tandem) to a corner point (with direction lines moving independently of one another). If you want one "face" of the corner point to be a standard anchor point, use the Subselection tool to drag its direction point into the corner point.

To change the size or shape of a curve—regardless of whether it passes through a smooth-curve point or ends at a corner point—simply drag its direction points. (Make sure to do this with the Subselection tool, not the Pen tool.) Each direction point acts like a magnet: When you move it away from the curve, the curve bends to follow it; when you move it toward the curve, the curve moves away from it (**Figure 14b**).

Figure 14b You can change the size or shape of a curve by dragging its direction points.

If you hold down the mouse button over the Pen tool icon in the toolbar, you'll see a menu showing several related tools:

- **Add Anchor Point.** This tool allows you to add a new anchor point between any pair of existing anchor points.

- **Delete Anchor Point.** This tool allows you to delete any anchor point from a path.

- **Convert Anchor Point.** This tool allows you to convert a smooth-curve point into a standard anchor point by clicking it. You can also convert a standard anchor point into a smooth-curve point by dragging outward from the point.

#15 Using the Selection Tools

You already know that the Selection tool (the black arrow) is used to select an entire path, and the Subselection tool (the white arrow) is used to select individual anchor points within a path. Here are other ways in which you might use selection tools:

- **Selecting more than one path.** Drag the Selection tool to outline a rectangular area on the Stage. When you release the mouse button, any paths within that area are selected. If a path is partly inside and partly outside the rectangular area, only the inside portion is selected.

- **Selecting more than one path on a crowded Stage.** You can use the Lasso tool to outline an irregularly shaped area surrounding the paths you want to select. When you release the mouse button, any paths within that irregular area are selected (**Figure 15a**). If a path is partly inside and partly outside the area, only the inside portion is selected.

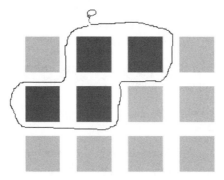

Figure 15a Outlining an area with the Lasso tool selects any paths (or portions of paths) within that area. The Lasso tool can't select individual anchor points.

- **Selecting more than one anchor point.** Drag the Subselection tool to outline a rectangular area on the Stage. When you release the mouse button, any anchor points that are within that rectangular area are selected, regardless of whether they belong to one path or several.

  Tip
  To select only one anchor point, draw a rectangle around it with the Sub-selection tool, which is often easier than trying to click the point itself.

- **Adding to an existing selection.** If one or more paths or anchor points are already selected, hold down the Shift key while clicking additional paths with the Selection tool, or anchor points with the Subselection tool. Those paths or anchor points are added to the selection.

- **Subtracting from an existing selection.** If multiple paths are already selected, hold down the Shift key while you use the Selection tool to click each path that you want to subtract.

- **Selecting everything.** Use the Selection tool to draw a rectangle around the entire Stage, or choose Edit > Select All.

- **Deselecting everything.** Use any of the selection tools to click an empty area of the Stage, or choose Edit > Deselect All.

#16 Using the Free Transform Tool

Transforming an object means changing its position, orientation, or proportions. Paths, groups (see #17), and symbol instances (see #23) can be transformed by means of the Free Transform tool.

You can use any of the methods described in #15 to select the objects that you want to transform. Alternatively, you can select objects directly with the Free Transform tool, either by clicking them or stretching a rectangle around them.

When you click the Free Transform tool in the toolbar, any currently selected objects become framed by a black rectangle. The rectangle has eight black squares (handles) around its perimeter—four at the corners, and four midway between each of them—that you can use to perform the transformations (**Figure 16a**).

Figure 16a The object inside this black rectangle is ready to be transformed. The pointer looks like a curved arrow, which means that dragging the mouse will rotate the object.

You can transform the selected object or objects in several ways:

- **Scaling.** Position your pointer directly on any of the eight handles. The pointer becomes a vertical, horizontal, or diagonal double-headed arrow. Depending on the orientation of the arrow, you can drag a handle vertically, horizontally, or both. (The top and bottom center handles adjust height, while the left and right center handles adjust width; the corner handles adjust both dimensions at once.) To scale the object without changing its ratio of width to height, hold down the Shift key while dragging a corner handle.

- **Rotation.** The white circle in the center of the rectangle is called the *transformation point;* it's the point around which the rotation will occur. (Think of it as a pushpin in the middle of a sheet of paper.) If you want to rotate the object around some point other than the center, move the transformation point to the desired spot. Place your pointer a few pixels outward from any of the corner handles. The pointer becomes a curved, double-headed arrow, indicating that you can now rotate the object clockwise or counterclockwise.

- **Skewing.** Skewing an object means changing the angles at the corners of the selection rectangle, making one pair of angles narrower and one pair wider, while keeping the sides of the rectangle parallel to each other. Place your pointer on the perimeter of the selection rectangle, midway between any two handles. The pointer turns into two overlapping half-arrows, indicating that you can now skew the object by dragging along the axis indicated by the arrows.

- **Distortion.** Distorting an object means moving each of its corner handles independently of the others. You can do this by holding down the Control key (Windows) or Command key (Mac) while dragging each corner handle individually. For a perspective distortion effect, do the same thing while holding down the Shift and Control keys (Windows) or Shift and Command keys (Mac) (**Figure 16b**).

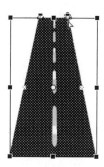

Figure 16b Tapering an object, otherwise known as distorting it in perspective, causes two sides of the selection rectangle to converge while the other two remain parallel.

#17 Grouping Objects

In #8 you found out how two identically colored fills can merge if they're allowed to overlap. Combining multiple objects into a single object is often desirable, but the problem with that method of merging paths is that it isn't reversible. When two or more paths are turned into one, they lose their identities as separate objects.

There are many occasions when you want to treat several objects as a single unit—for convenience in selecting them, for example—but want to retain the option to separate them again. In those situations, grouping is the answer.

To combine any number of objects into a single group, select them all and choose Modify > Group. This allows them to be selected with a single click (**Figure 17a**).

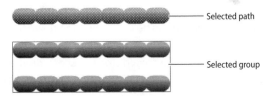

Selected path

Selected group

Figure 17a Unlike a path, which displays a dot-screen overlay when it's selected, a selected group is indicated by a blue rectangle.

A group doesn't behave like a path. Selecting a group and trying to change its fill color or stroke weight doesn't work. But if keeping the objects grouped becomes inconvenient, you can easily reverse the process by choosing Modify > Ungroup. All of the formerly grouped objects regain their independent identities, and they can once again be edited or transformed individually.

Often, you'll want to modify an object within a group, but you won't want to go through the trouble of ungrouping, making the modifications, and then grouping again. In such cases, you can edit objects within a group without ungrouping them.

To do this, choose the Selection tool and double-click the group on the Stage. Some odd things occur: The paths within the group now sport dot screens to indicate that they're selected and editable, and everything else on the Stage suddenly becomes dim. What's happened is that Flash has entered *group-editing mode.* Think of it as an alternate universe where the group is the only thing that exists.

To confirm that Flash is in group-editing mode, look at the narrow divider between the Timeline and the Stage. You'll see the phrase "Scene 1" on the left, and the word Group just to the right (**Figure 17b**). These words represent a type of navigation known as a *breadcrumb trail.* Each time you move from a wider environment to a narrower environment—for example, from the main Stage to the interior of a group or perhaps a symbol inside the group—your progress is charted from left to right on the breadcrumb trail.

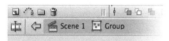

Figure 17b You know that you're in group-editing mode because the word Group appears at the end of the breadcrumb trail.

While you're in group-editing mode, you can make whatever changes you want to the objects in the group. Then, to find your way back to where you came from, follow the trail in reverse—that is, from right to left. In this case, if you want to exit group-editing mode, you can click "Scene 1", which represents the movie as a whole. The word Group disappears from the end of the breadcrumb trail; the group once again acts like a group; and all of the other objects on the Stage become accessible again.

Knowing how to follow the breadcrumb trail will become even more important when we get to #24, "Editing Symbols."

#18 Simplifying Objects

Keeping the size of the Flash file as small as possible is crucial, because the effectiveness of a SWF file depends partly on how quickly it can be downloaded from the Web.

The fewer the anchor points, the smaller the file is a good rule of thumb in working with vector graphics. If you can get rid of unnecessary anchor points, your animation will look better and play more snappily.

When you work with shape tools and primitive objects, extraneous anchor points are not a problem. But when you use tools such as the Pencil or Brush, you're likely to have many more anchor points than you need (**Figure 18a**). Every time your hand-drawn path jiggles or changes direction slightly, Flash creates another anchor point. Even if you use the Pen tool, you're often tempted to put in extra anchor points because it's easier than making smooth curves.

Figure 18a This path, drawn with the Pencil tool, has many more anchor points than it needs.

There are several ways to reduce the number of anchor points in a path:

- **Delete the anchor points manually.** If you're comfortable working with smooth-curve points, corner points, and direction lines, you can look for unnecessary anchor points in your path and use the Delete Anchor Point tool to remove them. This is time-consuming, but it gives you full control over the appearance of your paths.

- **Smooth your path.** You saw in #11 and #13 that the Smoothing controls in the Property inspector can make hand-drawn paths look much cleaner. In most cases, Flash removes unnecessary anchor points as part of the smoothing process. A smoothed path not only looks better; it also yields a smaller file size.

If you didn't use the Smoothing option when you created your path, you still can. Select the path with the Selection tool, then click the

Smooth icon in the options area of the toolbar (**Figure 18b**). You can click this icon repeatedly; each time you do, the path gets a little smoother. Another way to do the same thing is to select Modify > Shape > Smooth; you can do that repeatedly as well.

- **Optimize your path.** The automated way to simplify a path is to select the path and then choose Modify > Shape > Optimize. The resulting dialog box allows you to choose a degree of smoothing from None to Maximum. When you do so and click OK, Flash does the optimization and shows you the result, including a count of how many curves—essentially anchor points—were eliminated.

You'll almost always want to select "Use multiple passes (slower)" in the Optimize Curves dialog box. This option does slow down the process, but not drastically so, and it usually yields better results.

Unlike the Simplify command in Illustrator, the Optimize command in Flash offers no preview. The only way to find the best setting for a particular path is by trial and error. A good strategy is to start with the maximum and see what that does to your path. If the path is too distorted, you can undo the optimization and try it again with a slightly lower degree of optimization.

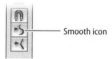

Smooth icon

Figure 18b Each time you click this icon, your selected path gets smoother.

#19 Working with Text

Most of your Flash movies will contain text of one kind or another. If you've ever used a word processor, you should be comfortable with the way Flash handles text.

To add text to the Stage, select the Text tool from the toolbar. The Property inspector fills up with options, the most important of which is the "Text type" menu on the left side. Make sure the menu says Static Text. (The other options—Dynamic Text and Input Text—are for specialized ActionScript applications.)

Use the Text tool to drag a rectangle across the Stage. Make the rectangle as wide as you want your text block to be, but remember that you can adjust the width at any time by dragging the white square at the upper-right corner of the rectangle (**Figure 19a**). A blinking cursor appears inside the rectangle, indicating that Flash is ready to accept your text entry.

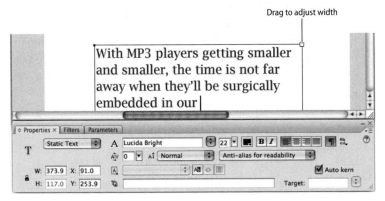

Figure 19a As you type, the text wraps to a new line when it reaches the right side of the rectangle.

Options such as font, size, color, alignment, and so forth should be self-explanatory. It's worth pointing out, however, that Flash allows the text size to be set dynamically by means of a slider. You can select a block of text and move the slider up and down until the size looks right.

When you include text in a movie, it's important to understand how Flash handles fonts. You can use a particular font only if that font is installed on the computer you're using. When you test or publish your movie, a subset of the font is embedded in the SWF file, so anyone who watches the movie will see the text in the correct font and size. However, *no* font information is embedded in a FLA file. If you give your FLA file to colleagues or clients, be sure their computers have the necessary fonts installed. Otherwise, they'll be prompted to choose replacement fonts when they open the FLA file.

Anti-aliasing is the process used by Flash and other programs to make text and images look smoother onscreen. The Property inspector in Flash CS3 includes a Font Rendering Method menu that lets you set anti-aliasing options for each text field you create. If the text you're creating will be put into motion, you'll generally want to choose "Anti-alias for animation." If the text will be static, you'll get better results with "Anti-alias for readability." If you use extremely small text, it will probably be most readable with no smoothing at all. In that case, you'd choose "Bitmap text (no anti-alias)."

The Fine Print

Keep in mind that text has to be easily readable on a computer monitor. You may have a super-sharp flat-panel monitor, but the people who watch your movie may be doing so on an old, blurry CRT. Out of courtesy to your audience, try to avoid ornate typefaces, tiny font sizes, and large or dense blocks of text.

#20 Breaking Apart Text

A block of text in Flash is known as a *text object*, which is a self-contained unit. If you move, resize, or delete a text object, all of its text is affected.

Sometimes you may not want your text to behave as a single object, though. For example, you may want to animate an explosion, scattering all the text onscreen randomly. To do this, you have to convert your text from a single object to many; in fact, every character needs to be a separate object.

The Break Apart command on the Modify menu is ideal for situations like this. Break Apart does different things in different situations. When applied to a text object that contains two or more characters, Break Apart turns each into a separately selectable object (**Figure 20a**).

Figure 20a From left to right: a selected text object, the same text with Break Apart applied once; the same text with Break Apart applied twice.

You can apply the Break Apart command a second time to the same text. Applying it once breaks the text object into individual characters; applying it a second time converts each character into an editable vector path. Using Break Apart in this way has advantages and drawbacks:

- **Advantages.** When text characters have been converted to vector shapes, the computer no longer needs a specific font installed to display the text. You can save your FLA file and pass it on knowing that the text will display correctly. Also, converted text characters can be edited like any other vector path, allowing you to experiment with interesting typographical effects (**Figure 20b**).

Figure 20b After being broken apart twice, text characters can be edited like ordinary vector paths.

- **Drawbacks.** Breaking text apart is irreversible: Individual characters can't be turned back into an editable text block. If you need to change the content, spelling, typeface, anti-aliasing, or any other characteristic of the text, you'll have to input it all over again. Also, converting each individual character to a vector path may add an excessive number of anchor points, bloating the file size.

#21 Using Multiple Layers

Every new FLA file begins with a single layer. You can see it in the left column of the Timeline, labeled Layer 1.

Practically speaking, you need only one layer to create a vector drawing. That's because every time you create a new object, Flash stacks it on top of the previous ones in the same layer. The position of an object in relation to the others in the stack is known as its *depth level*.

To change the depth level of a particular object, use the commands under Modify > Arrange. For example, let's say a cloud is behind a building, and you want it to be in front. You could accomplish this by selecting the cloud and choosing Modify > Arrange > Bring to Front (**Figure 21a**).

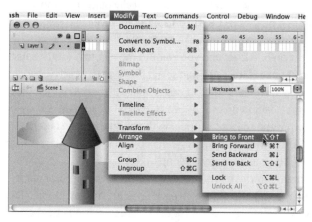

Figure 21a The Bring to Front command lets you bring an object up to the highest depth level.

The other commands on the Arrange submenu are Bring Forward, which moves a selected item up one depth level at a time; Send Backward, which moves the item down one depth level at a time; and Send to Back, which moves the item to the lowest possible depth level.

Using the Modify > Arrange commands can be tedious, especially if you have objects with different depth levels on one layer, so you may choose to distribute your objects among different layers.

Unlike Photoshop and Illustrator, each of which has a dedicated Layers palette, Flash displays all of its layers in the Timeline. To create a new layer in the Timeline, click the Insert Layer icon (**Figure 21b**). Each new layer is numbered by default, but you can change a layer's name by double-clicking the current name and typing a new one.

(continued on next page)

Voyage to the Bottom of the Stack

Unlike symbols (and symbol-like objects such as groups), editable paths don't have individual depth levels. Flash sends all paths on a layer to the bottom of the stack, regardless of when each path was created. If you ungroup a group, or break apart a symbol, any editable paths that were in the group or symbol lose their place in the stack and may no longer be visible. They haven't disappeared; they've just dropped to the bottom with all the other editable paths, where they may be hidden by other objects that are higher in the stack.

50

Good Housekeeping

If you're accustomed to working in Photoshop or Illustrator, you probably use layers freely, creating a new layer every time you want to add something new to your graphic. It's possible to do the same thing in Flash, but it's not common practice.

Because Flash is an animation program, objects often have to go on one layer or another for technical reasons. Using an unneeded layer makes editing your movie more confusing, so consolidate your objects onto one layer whenever possible. For example, if you have stationary objects in the background of your movie, it's best to put them all on a single layer (labeled "Background") instead of spreading them out over several layers.

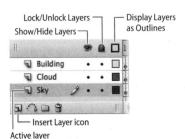

Lock/Unlock Layers ⌐ ⌐ Display Layers
Show/Hide Layers ⌐   as Outlines

⌐ Insert Layer icon
Active layer

Figure 21b Layer names are displayed in the leftmost column of the Timeline.

Once you have multiple layers in the Timeline, you have to keep track of which layer is active at any given time. The active layer is highlighted in blue. Any object that you create is automatically placed on the active layer. If you want a new object to be on a different layer, first select your preferred layer in the Timeline to make it active.

If an object is on one layer and you want to move it to another, select the object and choose Edit > Cut. Then select the layer to which you want the object moved and choose Edit > Paste in Place (if you want the object to have the same position on the Stage as it did before) or Edit > Paste in Center (if you want the object to appear in the middle of the Stage).

Layers that are higher up in the Timeline appear in front of layers that are lower down. You can drag any layer up or down.

There are three columns in the Timeline to the right of the layer names, and they affect the way the objects in each layer are displayed. Each has an "on" and an "off" setting; you can toggle between settings by clicking in the appropriate column and row.

The first column, with the Eye icon at the top, controls the visibility of each layer. A dot in column means the corresponding layer is visible; a red X means the layer is hidden.

The second column, with the Padlock icon at the top, controls the security of each layer. A dot in that column means the corresponding layer is unlocked; a padlock symbol means the layer is locked. No objects can be copied from, pasted to, or edited on a locked layer.

The third column, with the empty square at the top, controls the display mode of each layer. A filled square in that column means the layer is set to display strokes and fills; an empty square means the layer is set to display only unadorned paths. If you have a slow computer, turning off the display of strokes and fills may make the screen refresh faster and speed up your work.

Clicking the icon at the top of each column turns the corresponding setting on or off for all the layers.

CHAPTER THREE

Using Symbols and the Library

Most of the power of Flash comes from its ability to create and manipulate symbols. A *symbol* is a master object that resides in one place—a panel called the Library—but can generate multiple copies of itself that can be used anywhere in Flash. Symbols offer a variety of advantages:

- **Economy.** If you have a visible object that's intended to appear more than once in a Flash movie, you can convert it to a symbol. You can then place any number of instances (copies) of that symbol on the Stage without any significant increase in the movie's file size.

- **Adaptability.** Whenever you make a change in a symbol, that change is instantly reflected in all instances of the symbol.

- **Flexibility.** Every symbol has its own internal timeline. As a result, a symbol doesn't have to be static—it can be made to move or even to respond to a user's input.

- **Nestability.** Symbols can be embedded in other symbols, which can be embedded in still other symbols. By nesting symbols in this way, you can animate complex movements easily—for example, you could embed a symbol of a propeller turning inside a symbol of an airplane flying.

- **Scriptability.** Two kinds of symbols—buttons and movie clips—can be controlled by ActionScript. Movie clips can even include scripts of their own, allowing them to control other movie clips or the movie that contains them.

This chapter will show you the basics of creating, modifying, and organizing symbols. More advanced use of symbols will be covered in Chapter 4 ("Creating Animation") and Chapter 10 ("Using Basic ActionScript").

#22 Converting Objects to Symbols

Any object or group of objects that can appear on the Stage can be made into a symbol. Here's how to do it:

1. Select one or more objects on the Stage. The selected objects may include paths, text objects, bitmaps, or even other symbols.

2. Choose Modify > Convert to Symbol, or press the F8 key. The Convert to Symbol dialog box appears.

3. Type a name for the symbol into the Name field.

4. Click the radio button for the type of symbol you want to create: a movie clip, button, or graphic. (For the differences between these symbol types, see #27 and #28. If you're experimenting with symbols for the first time, the simplest choice is Graphic.)

5. Click one of the small squares in the diagram next to the word Registration. The square you click will determine the symbol's registration point (**Figure 22a**).

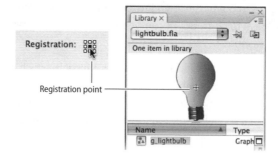

Figure 22a Click the square corresponding to your preferred location for the symbol's registration point. Later, when you view the symbol in the Library or in symbol-editing mode, your registration point will be indicated by crosshairs.

Think of the registration point as the handle by which Flash will hold the symbol when it's in motion (see #38). When you're in doubt, the center is usually a good choice.

6. Click OK.

You can find the symbol you just created in a panel called the Library. (If the Library isn't part of your current workspace, choose Window > Library.) When you click the symbol's name in the Library list, you'll see the symbol in the viewing pane above the list (**Figure 22b**).

Figure 22b Each symbol is listed in the Library next to an icon representing the symbol type. You can click the name of a symbol to see what it looks like.

It's also possible to create a symbol from scratch, without starting with an object on the Stage. To do so, choose Insert > New Symbol. You'll see a Create New Symbol dialog box.

When you complete the dialog box and click OK, Flash enters symbol-editing mode (see #24). If you wish, you can create some visual content for the symbol; if you'd rather wait until later, click Scene 1 in the breadcrumb trail to return to normal mode. If you don't create any content for the symbol, it will still be listed in the Library, but the viewing pane will be blank when you click the symbol's name.

(continued on next page)

Group or Symbol?

Let's say you have several objects on the Stage that you want to make selectable with a single click. Should you group them or convert them to a symbol? Here are some criteria to help you decide:

- **Impermanence.** If you want just to bring objects together temporarily, and you plan to separate them later, it's quicker to use a group than a symbol.

- **Uniqueness.** If a set of objects will appear only once in a movie, it's more efficient to group them than to convert them to a symbol.

- **Movement.** If you plan to animate a set of objects, convert them to a symbol. As you'll see in #38, both symbols and groups can be motion-tweened, but motion-tweening symbols is preferable.

Technically, Flash allows you to name a symbol whatever you like. In practice, you'll want to consider these issues when you choose a name:

- **Convenience.** Symbols listed in the Library can be sorted by name or by type, but it's much more convenient to have them sorted by name *and* by type without needing to switch between the two sorting modes. For this reason, many Flash developers like to give each symbol a prefix such as *b_* for button symbols, *g_* for graphic symbols, and *m_* for movie clip symbols. Doing so will cause the buttons, graphics, and movie clips to be gathered in separate groups in the Library's alphabetical listing.

- **Descriptiveness.** The more precise your symbol names are, the easier it will be to find the one you want among dozens or hundreds of symbols. If your movie contains graphic symbols of a beagle, a poodle, and a schnauzer, don't call the symbols g_dog1, g_dog2, and g_dog3. Instead, call them g_dogBeagle, g_dogPoodle, and g_dogSchnauzer. (Beginning all three of them with "dog" will cause them to follow each other in the Library's alphabetical listing.)

- **ActionScript compatibility.** If you're creating an interactive movie, you'll probably want to control your button and movie clip symbols with ActionScript. In that case, the names of your symbols will have to follow ActionScript's variable-naming rules. Make sure each symbol name begins with a lowercase letter. Having uppercase letters *within* a symbol name, as in g_dogBeagle, is fine. Also, make sure your symbol names contain only letters and numbers, with no spaces or punctuation other than an underscore.

Symboloids

In addition to symbols, Flash stores some items in the Library that are symbol-like but that don't fit the standard definition. They include:

- **Font symbols.** When Flash creates a SWF file, it automatically embeds font information for all the text characters that appear in the movie (see #19). But sometimes you'll want to embed font information for characters that *don't* appear in the movie, such as text that will be generated on the fly by ActionScript. To do so, you can right-click (Windows) or Control-click (Mac) anywhere in the Library list, choose New Font from the context menu, and select a font from a list of all the fonts installed in your computer. The font then appears as an item in the Library. Although embedded fonts don't behave like standard symbols, Flash occasionally calls them *font symbols*.

- **Components.** Flash comes with a collection of *components,* specialized objects that you can use to add interactivity to a movie (see Chapter 11). Components are initially stored in the Components panel, but once you drag a component into a movie, it appears in the Library as well. A component is in some sense a symbol (since it's an extremely refined type of movie clip), but it can't be edited or modified the way ordinary symbols can; only ActionScript can alter its appearance and behavior.

- **Multimedia assets.** When you import sounds, video clips, and bitmapped images into a FLA file, those assets are stored in the Library. They behave somewhat like symbols—for example, you can use multiple instances of them in your movie, and you can animate and transform those instances— but you can't modify multimedia assets inside Flash. Also, you can't change the color or opacity of instances of video clips and bitmaps unless you convert them to standard symbols.

#23 Working with Symbols and Instances

When you convert an object to a symbol, as you did in #22, the original object remains on the Stage. Although that object may look exactly as it did originally, it has become something quite different: It's now an *instance* of the symbol in the Library.

An instance is a marker that points back to a symbol and tells Flash, "display a picture of that symbol here." That's why multiple instances don't significantly affect file size: The symbol in the Library contains all the information that defines it and therefore takes up space in the file, but each instance contains barely any information other than a pointer to the symbol.

Note

Flash developers often refer to instances as symbols, as in "Let's remove that symbol from the Stage," but that's just shorthand. Strictly speaking, a symbol can be only in the Library; any copy of it on the Stage is an instance.

To create additional instances of a symbol, drag the symbol out of the Library and onto the Stage. The symbol itself stays in the Library; what gets dragged is actually an instance (**Figure 23a**). Another way to create additional instances is to duplicate an instance that's already on the Stage—by copying and pasting, for example.

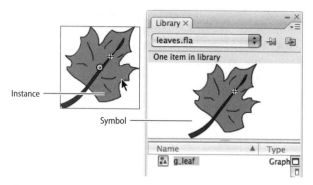

Figure 23a Every time you drag a copy of a symbol out of the Library, you've created a new instance of that symbol.

At first, all instances of a symbol look exactly the same as that symbol. It's possible, however, to change the appearance of an instance (**Figure 23b**):

- **Transformation.** By using the Free Transform tool, you can transform an instance in most of the same ways that you would a path: You can rotate it, scale it, or skew it (see #16). If an instance contains only vector paths, you can distort it as well.

- **Color effects.** When you select an instance on the Stage, a menu labeled Color appears in the Property inspector. You can change the instance's brightness, tint, or opacity by choosing the appropriate item from the menu (see #25).

Figure 23b All of these objects are instances of the same symbol. The one at the upper left is unaltered; the others have all been transformed or have had color effects applied.

When you alter an instance, you affect only that instance. The other instances and the symbol in the Library remain unchanged. In contrast, when you edit a symbol, the changes you make are reflected in all instances of that symbol (see #24).

Instance or Group?

Symbol instances and groups behave similarly on the Stage: Each allows you to select multiple objects with one click, as if they were a single object; each is surrounded by a blue rectangle when it's selected; and each becomes editable when it's double-clicked. (As you'll see in #38, each can be motion-tweened as well.) If you're not sure at first glance whether you've selected an instance or a group, there are two quick ways to tell: Look for the registration crosshairs (an instance has them; a group doesn't), or look at the Property inspector (it will say Group if a group is selected, or it will display the symbol type—Graphic, Button, or Movie Clip—if an instance is selected).

#24 Editing Symbols

There are two ways to edit a symbol. The first is to find the symbol in the Library and double-click either its name in the list or its image in the viewing pane. When you do so, everything on the Stage disappears, and the symbol you're editing becomes the only visible object. This is a good way to edit if you don't want to be distracted, but it prevents you from seeing the symbol in context with the other items on the Stage.

The second way to edit a symbol, called *editing in place,* is to double-click any instance of a symbol on the Stage. Flash goes into a symbol-editing mode that looks just like the group-editing mode described in #17: Everything other than the selected instance is dimmed, and the elements of the symbol become the only objects you can select and edit (**Figure 24a**). What's unusual about editing in place is that when you double-click the instance, it temporarily becomes *the symbol itself.* Any changes you make will affect not only that instance, but also all other instances of the symbol.

While you're in symbol-editing mode, using either editing method, you'll see a small white circle with crosshairs. That circle represents the symbol's registration point. The crosshairs can't be moved, but if you want to change the symbol's registration point, you can drag the contents of the symbol to a different position relative to the crosshairs.

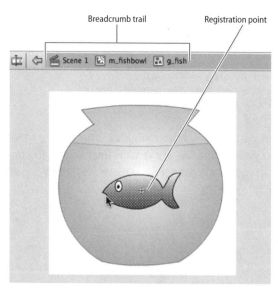

Figure 24a Flash is in editing-in-place mode for a graphic symbol called g_fish, which is inside a movie clip called m_fishbowl. The breadcrumb trail leads back to the original contents of the Stage.

If you have symbols nested within symbols, you can drill down one level at a time by editing the outermost symbol, then double-clicking a symbol embedded in it, and so on. You can return to any earlier level by clicking the appropriate link in the breadcrumb trail (see #17). Clicking the leftmost link, called Scene 1 by default, takes you back to the main Stage and exits symbol-editing mode.

Any changes you make to a symbol affect not only the symbol in the Library, but also all instances, even if they were placed on the Stage before you edited the symbol (**Figure 24b**).

Figure 24b Editing a symbol affects all instances of that symbol, even if they've been transformed or had color effects applied to them. (To see how these instances have changed, compare this screenshot to Figure 23b.)

The Domino Effect

When you edit a symbol, those changes affect all of its instances. The effects may be especially far-reaching if some of those instances are embedded in other symbols.

Say, for example, that an instance of Symbol A is embedded in Symbol B, and that an instance of Symbol B is embedded in Symbol C. If you make a change to Symbol A, the instances of *all three* symbols will reflect that change.

#25 Using Symbol Color Effects

Let's say you want to change the color of one instance of a symbol. You can't use the Color panel to change its stroke or fill, because an instance isn't editable. You can't double-click the instance and change its color in symbol-editing mode, because doing so would change the color of *all* instances of that symbol.

The solution is to select the instance and look for a menu marked Color at the right side of the Property inspector. From that menu—the Color Styles menu—you can choose the type of color effect you want to apply. Depending on which option you select, a different control (or set of controls) will appear next to the menu. The available options are:

- **Brightness.** The brightness control is a slider that goes from 100 percent to –100 percent, with 0 as the default. Choosing a positive number brightens the instance; choosing a negative number darkens it.

- **Tint.** There are several tint controls. The first is a standard Flash color menu that allows you to choose a tint for the instance in the same way you'd choose a color for a stroke or fill (see #9). Below the menu are three sliders—labeled R, G, and B—that allow you to adjust the individual levels of red, green, and blue on a scale ranging from 0 to 255.

  None of these tint controls discriminate between strokes and fills. As a result, tinting an instance causes the stroke and fill to appear the same color, even if they had contrasting colors to begin with.

  To avoid this, you can use the Tint Amount slider at the right of the color menu. This slider acts as if the tint were a separate object overlaying the instance: If the slider is set to 100 percent, only the tint is visible; if the slider is set to 0 percent, only the unchanged instance is visible. At intermediate settings—such as 50 percent, the default—the tint is treated as if it's partly transparent, allowing some of the underlying instance to show through. As you lower the tint amount, the original contrast between the stroke and fill colors becomes more apparent, but the tint looks increasingly washed out (**Figure 25a**).

Figure 25a The effects of the Tint Amount slider can be seen in these three different views of the same instance. On the left, the tint amount is set to 0 percent, leaving the original instance unchanged. In the center, the tint amount is set to 100 percent, completely covering the instance with a uniform color. On the right, the tint amount is set to 50 percent, allowing the instance to partially show through the tint.

- **Alpha.** This setting is synonymous with opacity. When the Alpha slider is set to 100 percent (the default), the instance is completely opaque; when it's set to 0 percent, the instance is completely transparent. If the background behind the instance is white, the effect of lowering the alpha is indistinguishable from raising the brightness.

- **Advanced.** This option lets you control tint and alpha at the same time. When you choose Advanced from the Color Styles menu, a button labeled Settings appears to the right. Clicking it brings up the Advanced Effect dialog box, which contains two columns of sliders.

  In the left column are RGB sliders and an Alpha slider. The Alpha slider works identically to the Alpha slider you saw earlier. The RGB sliders, however, work differently: Instead of making the stroke and fill the same color, they increase or decrease the amount of red, green, and blue by the *same percentage*, thereby preserving the differences between the stroke and fill colors.

  The sliders in the right column modify absolute amounts of red, green, blue, and alpha, in increments ranging from 255 to –255. Because they add the same amount to (or subtract the same amount from) each color, they preserve the differences between stroke and fill colors.

  For these reasons, if you use the Color Styles menu to change the color of an instance, you'll usually get better results with the Advanced option than you would with Tint.

#26 Breaking Apart Instances

As you've seen in #23 and #25, there are several techniques for modifying individual instances without changing the original symbol. Those techniques are limited, however. What if you *really* want to change the appearance of an instance—for example, by cutting a hole in it or changing its shape?

The answer is, you can't—at least not while the object you want to change is an instance. But it's possible to break the connection between an instance and a symbol, turning the instance into an independent, editable object. To do so, select the instance and choose Modify > Break Apart (**Figure 26**).

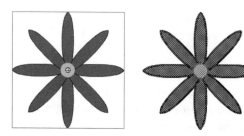

Figure 26 On the left, an instance of a symbol; on the right, the same instance after being broken apart. The dot screen indicates that it's now an editable object.

Keep in mind that using the Break Apart command has some negative consequences. When you break apart an instance, any color effects that you've applied to it disappear—since color effects work on instances only. Once an instance has been broken apart, it will no longer reflect changes you make to its parent symbol. And, most significantly, breaking apart an instance increases your movie's file size, since the former instance now contains real information instead of pointing to a symbol in the Library.

Think twice before you break apart an instance, because the process isn't reversible. Turning an editable object into an instance of an existing symbol isn't possible, although you can convert the object into a new symbol (see #22).

#**27** Creating Button Symbols

When users roll the pointer over a button, they expect it to respond in some way—by getting brighter, for example. This change in a button's appearance when a user rolls over it is known as a *rollover effect*.

When users click a button, they expect some feedback showing that their input has been recognized. This feedback may take the form of a sound (such as a beep or click), a change in appearance, or both.

Flash has made it easy to create buttons that provide all of these responses. Here's the usual procedure for making a functional button:

1. Use the drawing tools to create the button's normal appearance.

2. Select the paths that constitute the button and choose Modify > Convert to Symbol, or press F8. The Convert to Symbol dialog box appears.

3. Type a name for the button symbol (preferably with a *b_* prefix) into the Name field.

4. Under Type, choose Button.

5. Click a square to choose the registration point. For a button, the center is typical.

6. Click OK. The button symbol appears in the Library, and the button on the Stage becomes an instance .

7. Enter symbol-editing mode, either by double-clicking the button symbol in the Library or by double-clicking its instance on the Stage.

    You'll notice that the Timeline changes from its standard layout to a series of four cells labeled Up, Over, Down, and Hit (**Figure 27a**). The labels Up, Over, and Down refer to three variations, or states, of the button. The Up state is the button's appearance when the user isn't interacting with it; the Over state is the way the button looks when the user rolls the pointer over it; and the Down state is the way the button looks when the user is clicking it (**Figure 27b**).

(continued on next page)

The black dot in the Up cell indicates that the symbol that's currently on the Stage will represent the Up state of the button.

Figure 27a This is how the Timeline looks when a button symbol is being edited.

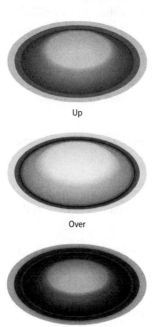

Up

Over

Down

Figure 27b These examples show how a button might look in each of its three states.

8. Click in the cell below the Over label. The cell darkens to indicate that it's selected.

9. Choose Insert > Timeline > Keyframe, or press F6. (To understand what's happening in this step, see #30.) A black dot appears in the Over cell.

10. Change the button's appearance to how you'd like it to look in its Over state. (The changes you make won't affect the button's appearance in the Up state.)

11. Repeat steps 8 through 10 in the next cell for the button's Down state. You can ignore the Hit cell for now.

12. Click Scene 1 in the breadcrumb trail above the Stage. Flash exits symbol-editing mode.

13. Choose Control > Enable Simple Buttons. (If the Enable Simple Buttons command already has a check mark next to it, skip this step.)

14. Roll your pointer over the button instance on the Stage. You'll see it change to its Over state.

15. Click the button instance on the Stage. While your mouse button is depressed, you'll see the button in its Down state.

While those are the basic steps for making a multistate button, there are other things you might want to do to enhance it. For example:

- **Add audio.** You can add sounds as well as images to the Over and Down states. To find out how to attach an event sound to a keyframe, see #61.

- **Add motion.** A button doesn't have to be static; any or all of its three states can be animated by means of embedded movie clips. To find out how to accomplish this, see #43.

(continued on next page)

- **Add a Hit frame.** Some buttons are difficult for a user to click—for example, because they're too small or irregularly shaped (**Figure 27c**). You can make the button more user-friendly by giving it a larger or more uniform "hot zone." To do so, return to editing the button and repeat steps 8 through 10 for the Hit cell. The variation of the button you use for the Hit frame won't be seen on the Stage, but it determines the size and shape of the clickable area around the button.

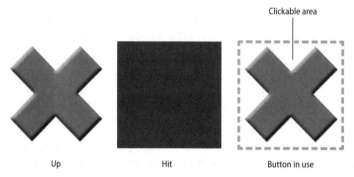

Clickable area

Up   Hit   Button in use

Figure 27c A button's Up state is on the left, and its Hit frame is shown in the center. The stroke and fill colors don't matter for the Hit frame; all that matters is the shape of the filled path. That path determines the button's clickable area, indicated by a dashed line on the right.

Although this button may be attractive and easy to use, it's still missing one important feature: It doesn't *do* anything. To make the button functional, you'll have to control it with ActionScript, which you'll find out about in #88.

#28 Comparing Graphic Symbols and Movie Clips

While button symbols are used for a single, specialized purpose, graphic symbols and movie clips have broader applications. Although *graphic symbol* sounds like something that contains a still image and *movie clip* sounds like something that contains motion, the truth is that either symbol can have either type of content. The differences lie elsewhere.

If you're creating a symbol and you don't know whether to make it a graphic symbol or a movie clip, consider these issues:

- **Dependent or independent?** Any instance of a graphic symbol is dependent on the pace of the movie it's placed in. If the symbol contains animation that takes 52 frames to complete, then you'll probably want the instance to remain on the Stage for 52 frames. If the movie ends before those frames have elapsed, the action in the symbol will be interrupted.

  In contrast, a movie clip runs independently of the movie it's in. As long as a movie clip is on the Stage, its animation will continue, even if the main movie ends (**Figure 28a**). For that matter, when the action in the movie clip reaches its end, it will start playing over again from the beginning and loop repeatedly—unless you deliberately stop it with ActionScript.

Figure 28a The rotation of this pinwheel is contained in a movie clip. Even after the animation of the child is over, the pinwheel will continue to turn.

(continued on next page)

- **Passive or interactive?** ActionScript can't control instances of graphic symbols—in fact, it doesn't even recognize that they're there. For that reason, graphic symbols are useful mostly for traditional animation, the kind that the user watches but doesn't interact with.

  In contrast, a movie can use ActionScript to control the movie clip instances within it, and any of those instances can use ActionScript to control any of the others. (In fact, many interactive movies are only one frame long. The action takes place not in the Timeline, but in sequential commands issued to movie clips by ActionScript.)

  The fact that a movie clip instance can be controlled by ActionScript doesn't mean it has to be. It's fine to have a movie clip that simply plays animation.

  In a situation where a graphic symbol or a movie clip would serve equally well, it makes sense to go with a graphic symbol since it will take up less space in the SWF file and make fewer demands on the computer's processor.

Tip

If you create a symbol as a movie clip and decide later that it should have been a graphic symbol—or vice versa—it's not too late. Select the symbol name in the Library list and click the Properties button (a lowercase I in a circle) at the bottom of the Library panel. A Symbol Properties dialog box appears in which you can rename the symbol and assign it a different symbol type.

#29 Using the Library to Manage Symbols

The Library is more than a repository for symbols; it's also a place where you can organize, modify, and track symbols. Many of the Library's features are hidden—either represented by small, unlabeled icons or listed on menus that are not immediately obvious (**Figure 29a**).

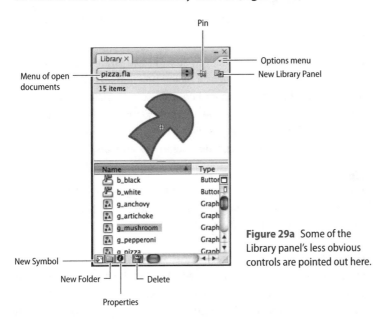

Pin

Options menu

New Library Panel

Menu of open documents

New Symbol

New Folder

Properties

Delete

Figure 29a Some of the Library panel's less obvious controls are pointed out here.

Let's look first at the four icons at the bottom of the Library panel. They are, from left to right:

- **New Symbol.** Clicking this icon brings up the Create New Symbol dialog box (see #22).

(continued on next page)

- **New Folder.** Just like the files on your computer's hard drive, the items in the Flash Library can be sorted into folders. Clicking the New Folder icon creates an empty folder into which you can drag any number of library items, including other folders. To see the folder's contents, double-click the folder in the Library list; to collapse the folder, double-click it again.

- **Properties.** When you select any item in the Library (other than a folder), clicking this icon opens a dialog box that lets you modify the item's properties. The name and contents of the dialog box depend on what type of item you've selected. For example, if you've selected a symbol, the Symbol Properties dialog box appears; if you've selected a sound file, the Sound Properties dialog box appears.

Tip
For Library items that can't be edited in Flash, such as bitmaps and sounds, another way to bring up the Properties dialog box is to double-click the item's icon in the Library list.

- **Delete.** You can delete any item in the Library by selecting it and clicking the Delete icon or pressing the Delete key. Be careful, however: If you delete a symbol, all instances of that symbol will vanish from the movie. If you delete a folder, Flash will delete everything contained in the folder without giving you a warning or asking for confirmation.

The two icons to the right of the Library list allow you to widen the Library panel (making all of the columns visible) and to narrow it again (**Figure 29b**). If the Library panel is docked, clicking the Widen icon not only widens the Library panel, but also widens the dock and all the other panels in it.

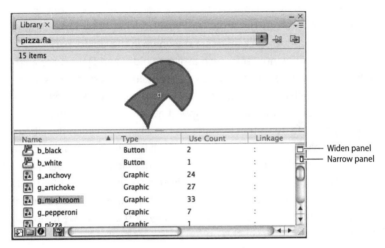

Figure 29b Widening the Library panel reveals previously hidden columns, including Use Count.

The remaining icons allow you to deal with multiple FLA files. If more than one document is open, the panel displays the Library contents of whichever document is in the foreground. To see the contents of another document's Library, you can select the document's name from the pop-up menu above the viewing pane.

The Pin icon to the right of that menu allows you to "pin" the current Library in place—that is, to keep the current document's contents visible in the Library panel even if you bring a different document to the foreground. Click the icon once to "pin" the Library; click it again to "un-pin" it.

The next icon to the right is the New Library Panel icon, which opens another copy of the current Library in a separate panel. Doing this can be useful if you want to drag items between panels to copy them from one Library to another.

(continued on next page)

Tip
If you copy an instance from the Stage of one FLA file and paste it to the Stage of another, the instance's parent symbol will automatically appear in the second file's Library.

Most of the Library's other features can be found in the Options menu, which you open by clicking the three-line icon at the upper-right corner of the panel. You can get an almost identical menu by right-clicking (Windows) or control-clicking (Mac) anywhere in the Library panel.

Some of the menu items, such as New Folder and Delete, are alternative ways to access features we've already looked at; others, such as Rename and Select Unused Items, are self-explanatory. Two menu items that need special explanation are those that deal with use counts.

Among the features that become visible when you widen the Library panel is a column called Use Count. For each item in the Library, the Use Count column tells you how many instances of that item have been used in the movie. By default, the numbers in this column are refreshed only when you choose Update Use Counts Now from the menu. If you want the use counts to be updated automatically, you can choose Keep Use Counts Updated; however, this option puts a noticeable drag on the program's performance.

CHAPTER FOUR

Creating Animation

If you've created artwork in Photoshop or Illustrator (or on paper, for that matter), you're accustomed to drawing in visual space. What you may not be used to is drawing in *time*.

Time is what makes animation possible. Animation isn't just cartoon characters running around; the term refers to any incremental change in visual elements over time. Text moving across the Stage is animation; so is a black-and-white photo that blossoms into color.

If you're planning to use Flash strictly as an ActionScript programming environment—for example, to make dynamic Web interfaces—you may think it's not important to know how to create animation. In Flash, however, Web interfaces or online applications *are* animation. (After all, the user's interaction with the computer takes place over time.) Whether you're an aspiring animator, game developer, or interface designer, you'll need to be familiar with the techniques in this chapter.

#**30** Getting to Know the Timeline

The Timeline is where you control how the objects on the Stage change over time. The vertical red line that crosses the Timeline is called the *playhead;* it marks the passage of time as it sweeps across the Timeline from left to right (**Figure 30**).

The Frame Name Game

Most Flash developers don't use precise terminology in their day-to-day work. For example, a frame and a keyframe are technically different things, but people typically refer to both informally as "frames," as in "Go to the frame in which the balloon explodes." Similarly, a cell in the Timeline is technically not a frame unless there's something in it, but in everyday conversation, people call empty cells "frames" all the time, as in "Extend that sequence to frame 128." For that matter, you may even hear the Stage itself referred to as a frame, as in "Move that cloud out of the frame." Most of these usages come from the world of traditional film and animation, where they're perfectly acceptable. On occasion, you'll see those informal uses of the word in this book as well, when doing so makes instructions or explanations more readable.

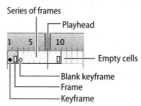

Figure 30 These are the features of the Timeline you'll use most often for animation.

The Timeline is divided into *cells,* each of which represents a unit of time. The duration of that unit varies according to the frame rate—see #31—but it's usually somewhere between one-twelfth and one-thirtieth of a second. The content of each cell (or each column of cells, if the Timeline has more than one layer) determines what's happening on the Stage at the moment the playhead passes over it.

The cells in the Timeline are empty by default, but you can fill them with either a keyframe or a regular frame.

- **Keyframe.** A keyframe signals to Flash that you want something in your movie to change. When the playhead passes over a keyframe, it updates the Stage to display whatever is new in that keyframe. A keyframe can also mark changes that aren't visible on the Stage, such as the start or end of a sound.

  To insert a keyframe into the Timeline, select the cell in which you want the keyframe to appear and choose Insert > Timeline > Keyframe, or press F6. A small black circle appears in the cell.

  On some occasions, you may want everything that was in the preceding keyframe to disappear. You can make this happen by choosing Insert > Timeline > Blank Keyframe, or by pressing F7. A blank keyframe is represented in the Timeline by a white circle instead of a black one.

- **Frame.** A frame (which we'll sometimes refer to as a *regular frame,* to distinguish it from a keyframe) signals to Flash that you want to maintain the status quo. When the playhead passes over a regular frame, it tells the Stage to continue displaying whatever was in the most recent keyframe.

To insert a frame into the Timeline, select the cell in which you want the frame to appear and choose Insert > Timeline > Frame, or press F5. A white rectangle appears in the cell.

To insert a *series* of frames, select the cell in which you want the series to end. (Flash will assume that you want the series to begin in the cell immediately following the most recent keyframe.) When you choose Insert > Timeline > Frame or press F5, a white rectangle appears in the last cell in the series. The intermediate frames don't contain white rectangles, but the dividing lines between the cells disappear; the absence of dividing lines is what allows you to distinguish a series of frames from a series of empty cells.

Note that you can't have empty cells in the middle of a movie. If you insert a keyframe, skip a bunch of cells, and then insert another keyframe, Flash automatically fills the intervening cells with a series of regular frames.

Note also that there may be different things happening on different layers. When the playhead reaches any given point in the Timeline—let's say it's frame 12—Flash looks at the entire column of cells and follows the instructions on each layer. For example, if frame 12 on Layer 1 is a keyframe, Flash will replace whatever was previously on that layer with whatever is new in that keyframe. If frame 12 on Layer 2 is a regular frame, Flash will continue to display whatever was in the previous keyframe in that layer. If frame 12 on Layer 3 is a blank keyframe, Flash will clear whatever was previously on that layer. All of these changes happen simultaneously when the playhead reaches a given frame, regardless of how few or how many layers there are.

Do It in Your Sleep

The three most commonly used function keys in Flash are almost certainly F5, F6, and F7, which insert a regular frame, a keyframe, and a blank keyframe, respectively. It's possible to accomplish these tasks via the Insert > Timeline menu options, but—apart from the newest of Flash beginners—nobody ever does. Particularly when you're doing frame-by-frame animation (see #32), which may require inserting dozens or hundreds of keyframes, you'd be downright crazy to use the menu. Get accustomed to those function keys now, and you'll never have to think about them again.

#31 Setting the Frame Rate

Every Flash movie has a *frame rate,* a measurement of how quickly the playhead moves through the Timeline. Frame rates are expressed in frames per second, usually abbreviated as *fps.* Flash permits frame rates ranging from 120 fps (the fastest) to 0.01 fps (the slowest), which is equivalent to 100 seconds per frame. For comparison, the standard frame rate for a theatrical film is 24 fps.

A movie's frame rate is displayed on the horizontal strip at the bottom of the Timeline (**Figure 31a**). The default frame rate is 12 fps, but you can change it by double-clicking the frame-rate display or by choosing Modify > Document.

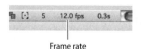
Frame rate

Figure 31a The frame rate of your movie is displayed here.

The smoothness of animation increases as the frame rate increases. For example, let's say the process of opening a door takes 1 second. You might animate the door opening in 10 frames at 10 fps, or you might animate it in 30 frames at 30 fps. Both animations would have a duration of 1 second, but the latter would be much smoother, because there would be less movement in each frame (**Figure 31b**).

Figure 31b If both of these sequences are played in the same amount of time, the bottom one will have a higher frame rate and thus will look smoother. If both sequences are played at the same frame rate, they'll look equally smooth, but the bottom one will have a longer duration.

A higher frame rate requires a larger SWF file (since more information has to be stored in the file), and it also puts more of a demand on the computer's processor. You'll often want to use a lower frame rate to gain efficiency at the expense of smoothness. If you're doing frame-by-frame animation (see #32), a lower frame rate also requires less work from you.

Keep in mind that the frame rate you set for a movie is only a target. For example, it's unlikely that a typical computer can play a movie at 120 fps. The lower you set the frame rate, the more likely it is that any given user will be able to see the movie as you intended. A frame rate of 12 fps is generally considered the minimum for acceptably smooth motion; most animation on the Web has a frame rate of about 15 fps.

When you set a frame rate, you set it for the entire movie; if you change it, you change it for the entire movie. You can't start a movie with one frame rate and end it with another—at least not without some tricky ActionScript. If you want to slow down a particular sequence in your movie, the optimal solution isn't to lower the frame rate, but to add more frames to the sequence.

Don't Be a Processor Hog

Since most computers are powerful enough to play animation at relatively high frame rates, why is the standard frame rate for Web animation no more than 15 fps? It's because computer processors usually have other things to do. For example, if you have three SWF files on a Web page and each one has a frame rate of 20 fps, the load on the user's processor is equivalent to that for playing a single SWF file at 60 fps.

The load factor is especially important to keep in mind if you're designing a Flash movie that users won't freely choose to see—for example, a banner advertisement. The frame rate for an ad should be 12 fps or lower, in order to leave lots of processor cycles available for the Web page's "real" content.

#32 Animating Frame by Frame

Background Check

If you want the background of your movie to be a solid color, there's no need to put a colored rectangle on a background layer. Instead, click anywhere on the Stage where there isn't a selectable object; doing so brings up Document Properties in the Property inspector. Use the Background menu to choose a background color for the Stage. Unlike using an object as a background, choosing a color from the Background menu is "free"—that is, it doesn't add to the size of the SWF file.

As you'll see in #36 and #38, Flash can automate mechanical kinds of motion through a process called *tweening*. But animation is most interesting when its motion *isn't* mechanical—when characters express their personality through the way they move (**Figure 32a**). To achieve that sort of expressive movement, you have to animate your characters one frame at a time. The basic procedure for frame-by-frame animation is short and simple:

1. In the Timeline, select the cell in which you want the animation to begin.

2. Press F7 to insert a blank keyframe.

3. Draw the first frame of animation on the Stage.

4. Press F6. Flash inserts a new keyframe immediately after the first one and copies the contents of the first into the new keyframe.

5. Modify the drawing on the Stage to represent the next incremental movement.

6. Repeat steps 4 and 5 as many times as necessary.

Figure 32a A character's idiosyncratic way of moving can be captured only by drawing it frame by frame.

Naturally, elements that stay the same from one frame to the next don't have to be redrawn in each new keyframe. Instead, put them on a separate layer in the Timeline (**Figure 32b**).

Figure 32b Because the drawing in each frame is slightly different from the previous one, frame-by-frame animation appears in the Timeline as a series of keyframes. Static background images should be put on a separate layer.

Each time you draw a new frame of animation, you'll want to make sure it flows smoothly from the frames that precede it. To do this, you can grab the pink rectangle at the top of the playhead and drag it back and forth through the Timeline at varying rates of speed—a procedure called *scrubbing*. As you scrub, the corresponding frames of animation play back on the Stage. Scrubbing often reveals slight glitches in the animation that you can then fix.

Once you have enough keyframes placed, you'll want to preview the animation at its proper frame rate, in any of these ways:

- Press Enter (Windows) or Return (Mac) to start the playhead moving through the Timeline. Press the same key to stop it. To move the playhead back to the beginning of the Timeline, press Control-Alt-R (Windows) or Command-Option-R (Mac).

- Make the Controller panel visible by choosing Window > Toolbars > Controller. The Controller offers a standard set of buttons for playing, stopping, and rewinding the movie.

- Use the menu commands Control > Play, Control > Rewind, and Control > Go to End.

In none of these cases do you have to stop the playhead manually. As soon as the playhead passes through all the frames and encounters empty cells, it knows it's at the end of the movie, and it stops on its own.

You can also generate a sample SWF file to test your movie (see #35).

Flash Isn't Creative: You Are

Before computers, animators drew one frame at a time. You'd think that powerful software such as Flash would relieve us of that drudgery, but in reality, most animation—at least most character animation—is *still* made one frame at a time. In fact, an animator's job has been much the same for over a century: Watching how people and things move in the real world, breaking down that motion into incremental steps, and trying to reproduce it in a series of images.

In old photos of animation studios, there were always mirrors on the wall. They allowed the animators to model the movements they were animating. If a character had to jump, the animator would jump in front of a mirror to see how his body moved. He'd then sketch it out back at his drawing table.

Frames of animation no longer have to be pencil-sketched, traced in ink, and hand-colored. But the humor, interest, and excitement of animation still come entirely from human creativity, frame by frame by frame.

#33 Onion Skinning

Even the most experienced animators often need help in creating smooth motion. The help in this case is a technique called *onion skinning*, which lets you draw each new frame of animation directly on top of images of previous frames. (The images are dimmed—more so for the earlier ones—to make it possible to draw over them without getting confused about what's new and what's old.)

To use this feature:

1. Move the playhead to the keyframe in which you want to make a new drawing.

2. Click the Onion Skin icon to turn onion skinning on. The playhead is now bracketed by two markers—Start Onion Skin and End Onion Skin—with a dark gray area between them (**Figure 33a**).

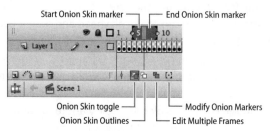

Figure 33a The onion skinning controls are above and below the Timeline.

By default, the Start Onion Skin marker is two frames behind the playhead, and the End Onion Skin marker is two frames after the play-head. (If there are fewer than two frames available in either direction, the markers move in toward the playhead as necessary.) To see more or fewer frames, slide the markers.

The frames bracketed by the markers are visible on the Stage, with increasing degrees of dimness depending on their distance from the playhead (**Figure 33b**).

Figure 33b This is how the Stage looks when onion skinning is turned on. The black stroke in the center is what's in the current frame. The dimmer strokes indicate what's in the two frames before and the two frames after.

3. Create or modify the drawing in the current keyframe, using the dimmed images for reference.

4. Press F6 to insert a new keyframe, or move the playhead to another keyframe. The Start Onion Skin and End Onion Skin markers move with it, keeping the same distance from the playhead.

5. Repeat steps 3 and 4 as many times as necessary. When you're finished, click the Onion Skin marker again to turn off the feature.

Here are some variations:

- To see just the paths in the onion-skinned frames, without strokes and fills, click the Onion Skin Outlines icon.

- If you want the ability to edit all the frames between the markers—not just the one that the playhead is positioned on—click the Edit Multiple Frames icon.

- To change the behavior of the markers—for example, to keep them visible even when onion skinning is turned off—click the Modify Onion Markers icon and choose one of the listed options.

The Skinny on Skinning

The term *onion skinning* has nothing to do with peeling vegetables. It comes from the early days of animation, when animators used to do their pencil sketches on semi-transparent paper called *onionskin*. To draw each new frame of animation, the animator would lay a sheet of onionskin paper on top of the previous one. The transparency of the paper allowed him to line up the new drawing with the old one and to trace portions when necessary. To test the animation, the animator would lift the corner of the stack of onionskin sheets and slowly release them with his thumb, watching the animation play frame by frame as each sheet of paper dropped into place.

#34 Editing in the Timeline

Once you've created and previewed an animated sequence, you'll almost always decide to go back and modify it. You may want to make parts of it longer or shorter, change its position in the Timeline, add more action to it, or take some action away.

We won't try to give you an exhaustive list of menu commands and keyboard shortcuts for editing; you can get that information from the Help menu. Instead, here are some general hints to help you deal with the less-intuitive aspects of working in the Timeline. (Note that any hints dealing with F6 apply to F7 as well.)

- If you want to insert a new keyframe between two existing keyframes, don't select one of the keyframes and press F6. (All that happens is that the playhead moves to the next keyframe; there are no changes at all in the Timeline.) Instead, select the first of the two keyframes and press F5 to insert a regular frame after it. The second of the two keyframes, and everything beyond it, moves one frame to the right. Then select the newly inserted frame and press F6 to turn it from a regular frame to a keyframe.

- If you want to delete a selected keyframe, don't choose Modify > Timeline > Clear Keyframe. That menu command and its keyboard shortcut, Shift-F6, will turn the keyframe into a regular frame instead of deleting it. Instead, choose Edit > Timeline > Remove Frames or press Shift-F5 to delete the selected keyframe.

- If you want to move a keyframe to another location in the Timeline, don't try to click it and drag it in one motion. Although this technique works in most programs, it doesn't work in the Flash Timeline—all you'll end up doing is selecting a series of frames. Instead, click the keyframe to select it; release the mouse button; then click again to drag the keyframe.

- If you want to paste frames from one part of the Timeline to another, don't use the standard Edit > Cut, Edit > Copy, and Edit > Paste menu commands or their keyboard shortcuts. Those commands work only for objects on the Stage, not for frames in the Timeline. Instead, use the special commands Edit > Timeline > Cut Frames, Edit > Timeline > Copy Frames, and Edit > Timeline > Paste Frames.

- If you have a series of regular frames at the end of your movie and you want to extend the series farther into the Timeline, don't select the last frame in the series and drag it; if you do, Flash may insert a keyframe after it. Instead, click the cell where you want the series to end and press F5. The series of frames will extend to meet the cell you selected.

- Similarly, if you want to shorten a series of regular frames (that is, have it end sooner), don't select the last frame in the series and drag it backward. Instead, find the frame that you want to end the series, click the frame immediately following it, and Shift-click the current last frame in the series. Then choose Edit > Timeline > Remove Frames, or press Shift-F5, to delete the selected frames.

- To extend a portion of a movie and keep all of its layers in sync, select a block of frames by clicking the frame at the upper-left corner and Shift-clicking the frame at the lower-right corner (**Figure 34**). Then drag the whole block of frames at once.

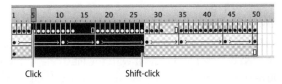

Click   Shift-click

Figure 34 You can select a block of frames across multiple layers.

Speaking Span-ish

If you choose Edit > Preferences (Windows) or Flash > Preferences (Mac), select the General category, and look under Timeline, you'll see one of the more obscure options in Flash: "Span based selection." If you turn it on, the Timeline treats any series of regular frames (including tweens) as a single unit called a *span*. Clicking any frame within the span selects the entire span.

This was how the Timeline worked in early versions of Flash, and many users found it confusing, because there was no obvious way to select a single frame. Starting in Flash 5, the Timeline changed to its current default behavior, but span-based selection remains an option for those who appreciate the convenience of selecting multiple frames with a single click.

#35 Testing the Movie

In #32, you learned several ways to preview your movie in Flash. All of these techniques have a drawback, however: They don't show you what the users' experience will be when they watch your movie. When you watch the movie in the Flash authoring environment, it usually runs more slowly than it would outside, because Flash has to do so many other things at the same time (such as animating the playhead as it moves across the Timeline). Also, you see things in the Flash environment that your users can't see, such as where objects go when they leave the Stage.

In contrast, the people who see your movie most likely won't even own Flash; they'll be playing it in their Web browsers using the Flash Player plug-in. To see the movie the way your users will see it, you too will have to preview it in the Flash Player. There are two ways to do this—one is more convenient, the other is more authentic.

The more convenient way is to choose Control > Test Movie, or press Control-Enter (Windows) or Command-Return (Mac). Flash generates a SWF file and opens it in a separate window representing the Flash Player. It's not *really* the Flash Player—it's actually a Flash Player module that's built into your Flash application—but it still gives you a reasonably good idea of what your users will see.

The more authentic way is to choose File > Publish Preview > Default. As with Test Movie, Flash generates a SWF file, but then it opens it in your computer's default Web browser and plays it with the Flash Player plug-in. In this case, you're seeing the same SWF file your users will see, under basically the same conditions.

Because the Test Movie command is so much quicker, you'll probably want to use it when you're first developing a movie. It's only when you bring your movie into its final stages, and begin to refine and polish it, that the difference between Test Movie and Publish Preview becomes important.

Loopy Behavior

When you preview your SWF file, no matter which method you use, you'll notice that your movie doesn't play just once—it repeats indefinitely, snapping back to the first frame as soon as it gets to the last. This looping is useful in that it gives you the opportunity to observe your movie carefully; but it's also a reminder that the movie will be looping when your users see it. (There are ways for you to prevent it from looping—an unreliable way using Publish Settings, covered in #78, and a reliable way using ActionScript, covered in #87—but the default behavior is to loop.) If you want to improve the users' experience, look for a creative way to smooth out the transition between the end of the movie and the beginning.

Creating Animation

#36 Creating Shape Tweens

Thanks to a process called *tweening*, not all animation has to be drawn frame by frame. If you give Flash two keyframes—one showing the way an object looks at the start of a sequence, and the other showing what it looks like at the end—Flash can compare the keyframes, analyze all the differences between them, and gradually change one to the other by generating a series of in-between frames.

There are two kinds of tweens: shape and motion. Here and in #37 we'll be concentrating on shape tweens, but much of how you handle shape tweens will also apply to motion tweens, which are covered in #38.

These are the basic steps for setting up a shape tween:

1. Draw an object on the Stage in an empty keyframe. Don't group the object or convert it to a symbol. Shape tweens work only with editable paths, primitive shapes, or Drawing Objects.

2. Decide on a duration for the shape tween and calculate in which cell of the Timeline the last keyframe should fall. (For example, if your frame rate is 15 fps, and you want the tween to take 3 seconds, the last keyframe should be 45 frames after the first keyframe.) Select that cell.

3. Press F6. Flash fills the in-between cells with regular frames, creates a new keyframe in the selected cell, and copies the object from the preceding keyframe into it.

4. With the second keyframe still selected, modify the object. You can reshape it, move it to a different place on the Stage, transform it with the Free Transform tool, change its color or opacity, or do any combination of those things.

5. Select the first keyframe again. (This will also work if you select one of the intermediate frames, but selecting the first frame is recommended.)

6. In the Property inspector, choose Shape from the Tween menu (**Figure 36a**). The frames between the two keyframes turn green, and an arrow points from the first keyframe to the last. The arrow is your confirmation that you have a working shape tween.

(continued on next page)

Arrow indicating tween

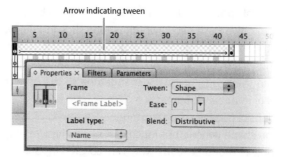

Figure 36a Choosing Shape from the Tween menu causes the two keyframes to be connected by a rightward-pointing arrow on a green background.

7. Scrub through or preview the movie. You'll see that in each tweened frame, the object in the first keyframe incrementally takes on the characteristics of the object in the second keyframe (**Figure 36b**).

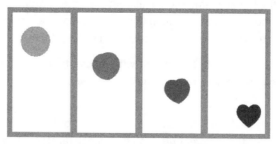

Figure 36b Shape, location, transformation, color, and opacity can all be tweened at once.

Shape tweens can be wild or tame (**Figure 36c**). Wild shape tweens are fun to watch because of the interesting patterns they produce; tame shape tweens are better for more realistic types of movement.

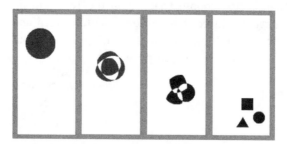

Figure 36c Figure 36b was an example of a tame shape tween; here is an example of a wild one.

If wild shape tweens are what you want, here are some things to try:

- Make the object in the first keyframe and the object in the second keyframe as different as possible. In fact, instead of pressing F6 in step 3, you can press F7, draw an entirely new object in the second keyframe, and then watch how Flash tweens one into the other.

- Have different numbers of objects in the two keyframes. This sort of tween is especially common with text—for example, morphing the word NO (two objects) into YES (three objects). Keep in mind, though, that if you want to shape-tween text, you first have to break it apart into editable paths (see #20).

If you prefer tame shape tweens—as most serious animators do—consider the following suggestions:

- Tween only one object per layer. Remember that Flash considers the stroke and the fill to be separate objects. If your path has both, move the stroke and the fill to different layers, and tween them separately but simultaneously (**Figure 36d**). Alternatively, you could use a Drawing Object, in which Flash considers the stroke and fill to be part of a single object.

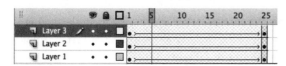

Figure 36d It's fine to have several shape tweens happening simultaneously on different layers.

- Simplify each object as much as possible. The fewer anchor points there are, the smoother the tween will be.

- Use shape hints, which are explained in #37.

Just Call 'Em Moshape Tweens

The words *shape* and *motion* are not very useful descriptors for the two kinds of tweens. Many Flash beginners reasonably assume that a shape tween is for changing an object's shape, and a motion tween is for moving an object around the Stage. Though it's true that only a shape tween can morph an object, both types of tween can put an object in motion, as well as change its size, orientation, color, and opacity. The main difference between the two tweens is not what they can do, but what they can do it *to*. Shape tweens work on editable paths and primitive shapes; motion tweens work on groups, symbols, and some of the "symboloids" described in #22. Drawing Objects can be tweened by either method.

#37 Using Shape Hints

Shape tweens are notoriously unpredictable. It may be clear to *you* what the most logical way is to morph one object into another, but that doesn't mean it's apparent to Flash. Even a simple transformation may take place in a way you don't expect (**Figure 37a**).

Figure 37a When a circle morphs into a square, we'd expect the four corners of the square to sprout directly from the circle. Instead, Flash rotates the circle as it becomes a square.

To help with this issue, Flash provides tools called *shape hints*. Shape hints always come in pairs: one to mark a point on a path in the first keyframe of a tween, the other to mark the corresponding point on the path in the second keyframe. You can use shape hints as follows:

1. Select the first keyframe of the tween.

2. Choose Modify > Shape > Add Shape Hint. A red circle with the letter *a* on it appears in the center of the object.

3. Drag the shape hint to the first point you want to mark—in this case, the upper-left edge of the circle. When you release the shape hint, you should see it snap into place (**Figure 37b**).

   If there's no obvious snap, it means you may not have dragged the shape hint fully onto the path. Try dragging it and dropping it again.

Figure 37b Snap the first shape hint to the first object in the tween; then snap the second shape hint to a corresponding point on the second object.

4. Select the second keyframe of the tween. An identical red circle with the letter *a* on it is in the center of the object.

5. Drag this second shape hint to the point that corresponds to the point you marked in step 3—in this case, the upper-left corner of the square. Once again, let it snap into place.

   If everything has been done correctly, this shape hint should turn from red to green, and the first shape hint should turn from red to yellow. If the shape hints are not yet yellow and green, repeat the drag-and-snap process until they are.

6. Preview the movie to see whether the shape tween now does what you want. In many cases it won't; often one pair of shape hints is not enough (**Figure 37c**).

Figure 37c Even after we add shape hints, Flash still doesn't get it.

   If necessary, repeat the process to add a second pair of shape hints (**Figure 37d**). Flash labels the second pair with the letter *b,* the third with *c,* and so on.

Tip
If you add multiple shape hints, it's best to start in the upper-left corner of the object and then to work counterclockwise. Keep the shape hints in order around the perimeter of the object.

Figure 37d When adding shape hints, work in a counterclockwise direction from the upper-left corner.

(continued on next page)

In the example of the circle morphing into the square, two pairs of shape hints is sufficient (**Figure 37e**). In other cases, more may be needed.

Figure 37e Adding the second pair of shape hints solves the problem.

In general, if five or six pairs of shape hints don't get you the result you want, it's unlikely that adding more will help. In that case, you might consider deleting the shape tween and trying a new one with simpler paths.

#38 Creating Motion Tweens

Creating motion tweens is very similar to creating shape tweens (see #36). Here are the significant differences:

- Motion tweens work only with groups, instances of symbols, and symbol-like objects such as bitmaps.

    ### Note
    Because groups and Drawing Objects are unique objects, rather than master objects in the Library with instances on the Stage, motion-tweening those objects sometimes leads to problems. If possible, convert groups or Drawing Objects into symbols before motion-tweening them.

- Motion tweens can change an object's location, transformation, color, and opacity, but they can't morph one object into another as shape tweens can.

- Unlike a shape tween, which can include multiple objects in a single keyframe, a motion tween works with one object at a time. If you want to motion-tween several objects simultaneously, each must be tweened separately on a separate layer.

- Motion tweens can be controlled by motion guides (see #40); shape tweens can't.

- Motion tweens are more predictable, more reliable, and less processor-intensive than shape tweens. If you have the option of using either a shape tween or a motion tween to achieve the same effect, use the motion tween.

Here are the usual steps for setting up a motion tween:

1. Place an instance of a symbol on the Stage in an empty keyframe.

2. Decide on a duration for the motion tween, and select the cell in which the last keyframe should fall.

3. Press F6. Flash fills the in-between cells with regular frames, creates a new keyframe in the selected cell, and copies the object from the preceding keyframe into it.

(continued on next page)

Tweaking Tweens

Both motion and shape tweens are easily adjustable. If the timing doesn't seem right, you can extend or shorten a tween by dragging either or both of its keyframes. Flash automatically adjusts the rate of change in the intermediate frames.

If you want to add more nuance to a tween—for example, you want an object to shift direction as it moves from one point to another, or you want the rate of change to increase midway through—you can add keyframes within a tween. Select any of the intermediate frames and press F6; then make whatever changes you want in the new keyframe.

Back in Black

It's a cinematic tradition to have the first scene of a movie fade up from a black screen, and the last scene fade to black. An easy way to achieve these effects in Flash is to create a graphic symbol of a black rectangle and to place an instance of it in the Timeline so it covers everything on the Stage. At the beginning of the movie, you can motion-tween the rectangle from full opacity to zero opacity, then do the opposite at the end.

For a motion tween to work, the objects in both keyframes must be instances of the same symbol.

4. With the second keyframe still selected, modify the object. You can move it to a different place on the Stage, transform it with the Free Transform tool, change its color or opacity, or do any combination of those things.

   To change the object's color or opacity, use the Color Styles menu (see #25). Changing color by means of swatches or the Color panel doesn't work with motion tweens.

5. Select the first keyframe again. As with shape tweens, the process will work if you select one of the intermediate frames, but selecting the first frame is recommended.

6. In the Property inspector, choose Motion from the Tween menu. The frames between the two keyframes turn blue (not green, as with a shape tween), and an arrow points from the first keyframe to the last.

7. Scrub through or preview the movie to see the motion tween in action.

#39 Troubleshooting Broken Tweens

Every so often when you create a tween, the Timeline fails to display the confirming arrow on a green or blue background; it displays a dashed line instead (**Figure 39a**). The dashed line indicates that there's something wrong with the tween. Although Flash notifies you that the tween is broken, it won't tell you *why*. Diagnosing and fixing the problem is left to you.

Figure 39a This dashed line indicates that a tween is broken.

Here are some common causes of broken tweens:

- You've tried to shape-tween groups or symbols, or you've tried to motion-tween editable paths.

- The beginning or ending keyframe of the tween is empty.

- In a motion tween, the object in the first keyframe and the object in the last keyframe are different.

- You've tried to motion-tween more than one object on a single layer.

The last of these causes is often the most frustrating, because it's not always obvious. At some point, without realizing it, you may have made a stray mark with the Pencil tool or failed to erase a path fully, leaving a tiny, unnoticeable object on the Stage. If such an object is hiding out in the first or last keyframe of a motion tween, the tween will fail, and you may never figure out why.

If you suspect that a barely visible object is what's breaking your tween, here's an easy way to solve the problem:

1. Move the playhead to the first keyframe of the tween.

2. On the Stage, select the object that's being tweened.

3. Choose Edit > Cut. The tweened object disappears.

4. In the Timeline, look at the color of the circle in the keyframe. If it's white, then the object you just cut was the only object in the keyframe. You can skip to step 7. But if the circle is black, it means that the keyframe isn't empty, and that there must be something else occupying the keyframe.

(continued on next page)

Boulevard of Broken Tweens

Because broken tweens are often difficult to diagnose and repair, many people ignore them. In some cases, even though Flash displays a dashed line in the Timeline, the tween seems to work anyway, so the animator leaves well enough alone. In other cases, when the tween doesn't work at all, the animator just conveniently forgets that there was a tween there in the first place.

It's never a good idea to leave a broken tween in a movie; the dashed line in the Timeline may be a sign of more fundamental corruption in the FLA file. If none of the suggestions here are effective, you might try the clean-slate approach: Delete the tweened material and rebuild that portion of the movie from scratch.

5. Click the keyframe in the Timeline to select all the objects in the keyframe.

6. Press Delete to clear the unwanted objects out of the keyframe. The circle in the keyframe turns white, indicating that the keyframe is empty.

7. Choose Edit > Paste in Place to return the original tweened object to the Stage.

8. Look at the tween in the Timeline. If the dashed line has been replaced by an arrow, you've solved the problem. If not, go to the last keyframe of the tween and follow steps 2 through 7 again.

#40 Using Motion Guides

When you tween an object from one location on the Stage to another, the tweened object moves in a straight line. If you want the object to follow a more interesting path, you can use a *motion guide* to steer it.

To create a motion guide:

1. Motion-tween an object from one point to another. (Motion guides don't work with shape tweens.) It doesn't matter where the object starts and ends; you'll adjust that later.

2. Select the layer in the Timeline that contains the tweened object, and click the Add Motion Guide icon (**Figure 40a**). A new layer appears, with the layer you selected indented beneath it.

   The new layer's icon indicates that it's a specialized type of layer called a *guide layer*. The layer containing your tweened object has become a *guided* layer.

Figure 40a   The Timeline looks like this when it contains a guide layer.

3. Select the empty keyframe at the beginning of the guide layer.

4. On the Stage, draw the path you'd like the tweened object to follow. You can draw it with any tool, but the Pencil or Pen is recommended.

(continued on next page)

Guidance Counselor

The technical requirements for a motion guide are loose: The path can be any length and any shape; it can be open or closed; and it can be drawn with any tool. However, there are some things you can do to make a motion guide more effective and easier to use:

- Make sure the motion guide is a single path with no gaps.

- Simplify the path as much as possible. Use the Smooth or Optimize commands to get rid of sharp corners and unnecessary anchor points.

- Don't allow the path to cross over itself.

- Lock or hide the guide layer when you're working on other parts of the movie. (The motion guide functions even if it's locked or hidden.)

5. Drag the tweened object to one end of the motion guide and snap it to the guide (**Figure 40b**).

    The snapping maneuver is tricky. Try to drag the object by its registration point and drop it a short distance inward from the beginning of the path.

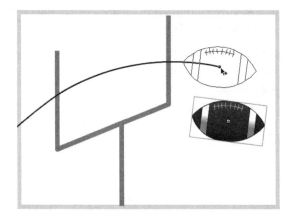

Figure 40b The registration point of a symbol instance is marked with a white circle. Grab the instance by that circle, and drop the circle precisely onto the motion guide.

6. Drag the playhead to the last keyframe of the tween and snap the object to the other end of the motion guide.

7. Scrub through or preview the movie. Instead of traveling in a straight line, the tweened object should follow the motion guide. If it doesn't, try repeating steps 5 and 6 a few more times.

8. By default, the tweened object maintains the same orientation no matter where it moves along the path. If you'd prefer that the object vary its orientation, always staying perpendicular to the portion of the path it's on, select Orient to Path in the Property inspector.

#41 Masking

A *mask* is something that hides one part of an object and exposes another part of the object. Creating a mask is simple:

1. Place the object to be masked on one layer, and the object that will act as a mask on the layer just above it.

    The mask can be a path, a Drawing Object, a group, an instance of a symbol, a block of text, or just about anything else. Its stroke and fill colors don't matter (**Figure 41a**).

Figure 41a Top, a mask (the text) and an object to be masked. Below, the same objects after the Mask command has been applied.

2. Right-click (Windows) or Control-click (Mac) the name of the layer containing the mask, and select Mask from the contextual menu.

    Flash converts the upper layer into a mask layer and the lower layer into a masked layer. The object on the Stage appears masked.

Note
Flash locks the mask layer and the masked layers because that's the only way the mask effect can be seen within Flash. If you unlock either layer, the effect disappears. In the SWF file, the mask effect is always visible, regardless of whether the layers in the FLA file are locked or unlocked.

(continued on next page)

A mask on its own is no big deal. What makes masks interesting is that you can animate the mask, the masked object, or both, thereby achieving complex effects quickly (**Figure 41b**).

Mask layer

Normal layer | Masked layer

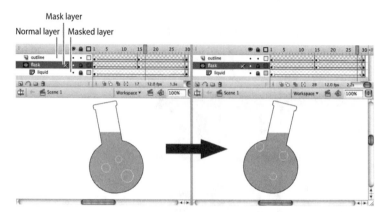

Figure 41b The bubbles in the water are shape-tweened paths; the laboratory flask is a motion-tweened instance of a symbol. The animated flask is used to mask the animated water, allowing the water level to stay the same no matter which way the flask is tilted.

It's possible to have one mask layer affect multiple masked layers. If there's a layer that you want to put under the control of an existing mask, drag and drop it between a mask layer and a masked layer in the Timeline (**Figure 41c**). The masked layers can be arranged in any order, so long as the mask layer is above them all.

Figure 41c In this Timeline, one mask layer is affecting two masked layers.

Creating Animation

#**42** Copying and Pasting Motion

It's always been possible to copy and paste animation from one part of the Timeline to another. One of the new features in Flash CS3 goes a step beyond that: It allows you to copy animation from one object and apply it to another.

Let's say, for example, that you're animating three different cars, each one starting from a different place on the Stage. You want each car to go straight, make a left, make a right, and roll over. In previous versions of Flash, there was no easy way to do this without using ActionScript, but in Flash CS3 it can be done in a few seconds:

1. Create graphic symbols for all three cars and put each one in its proper place on the Stage.

2. Motion-tween the first car.

3. Select the first car on the Stage and choose Edit > Timeline > Copy Motion.

4. Select the second car on the Stage and choose Edit > Timeline > Paste Motion.

5. Repeat step 4 for the third car.

When you copy animation from one object and paste it to another, the motion is relative to the *object*, not to the Stage. As a result, each car can execute the same set of maneuvers in completely different locations.

There are a couple of potential problems that you'll need to be alert for. Imagine that the second and third cars are both in the same keyframe on the same layer. That's fine, so long as they're standing still. But as soon as you paste the first car's motion to the second car, you've turned the second car into a motion-tweened object; as you'll remember from #38, a motion-tweened object has to be on a layer of its own. So you'd have to move the second and third cars to separate layers before you could paste motion to them.

(continued on next page)

Similarly, suppose the first car's animation has a duration of 100 frames, but the second and third cars are in the movie for only 50 frames. When you paste the first car's motion to the second car, Flash will automatically lengthen the second car's span by 50 frames. If there's any action in the Timeline that's later in the same layer, that action will be delayed by 50 frames, possibly losing coordination with the action in the other layers (**Figure 42a**).

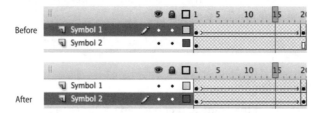

Figure 42a These two views of the Timeline show what happens when motion from Symbol 1 is pasted to Symbol 2.

#43 Putting Animation Inside Symbols

Whenever you're in symbol-editing mode, you might notice that all of the information in the Timeline disappears. That's because when you edit a symbol, you stop seeing your movie's Timeline and start seeing that *symbol's* timeline. Every symbol in Flash has its own internal timeline. (As you saw in #27, the one inside button symbols is greatly simplified, but it's a timeline nonetheless.)

The significance of symbol-specific timelines is that they allow you to put animation *inside* a symbol. Because instances of symbols appear in a movie's Timeline, and because instances of other symbols may appear in a symbol's timeline, it's possible (and actually common) to have several different levels of animation going on at once.

For example, suppose you want to animate a person running across the Stage. If you had to do this frame by frame, it would take you forever, but the use of animated symbols streamlines the process.

Here's all you'd have to do:

1. Create a new movie-clip symbol and give it a descriptive name such as m_running.

2. Go into symbol-editing mode and animate the running person within m_running's timeline (not in the movie's Timeline).

   You need only animate one cycle (that is, left foot forward and right foot forward). Make the cycle smooth enough that it can loop repeatedly without it being apparent where the cycle begins and ends (**Figure 43a**).

Figure 43a This frame-by-frame animation was created inside a movie-clip symbol.

3. Drag an instance of m_running onto the movie's Stage.

4. Motion-tween the instance to make it travel across the Stage.

(continued on next page)

When you design buttons that provide user feedback (see #27), it's sometimes appropriate to include animation—for example, to make a button flash on and off when a user rolls over it. In theory, that should be easy, except buttons don't contain ordinary timelines: They have a specialized timeline containing only four frames, which isn't suitable for animation.

The solution is to put the animation inside a movie clip, because, as described in #28, once a movie clip starts playing, it loops indefinitely. So a movie clip is the perfect type of symbol to use inside a button symbol. If you put the movie clip into a single frame of a button's timeline—the Over frame, for example—the movie clip will start to play when the user rolls over the button, and it will keep playing until the user clicks the button or rolls off it.

5. Test or preview the movie. You'll see two levels of animation going on at once: the animation within the symbol of the person running in place, and the animation outside the symbol of the running person moving across the Stage (**Figure 43b**).

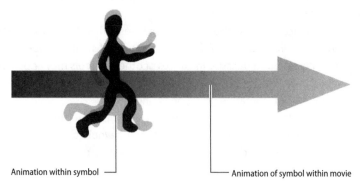

Animation within symbol ⌐   ⌐ Animation of symbol within movie

Figure 43b   As this person runs across the Stage, two levels of animation are going on at once.

Placing animation inside symbols is powerful and convenient, especially if you're creating an interactive movie in which the action is different every time. The Timeline for many interactive movies is only one frame long, because all of the movie's possible animation is contained within the symbols in the Library.

#**44** Working with Scenes

Scenes are a prominent part of the Flash interface. There's a Scene panel; there's an Edit Scene menu (identified by a clapper board icon) right above the Timeline; and whenever you're in group- or symbol-editing mode, you follow the breadcrumb trail back to Scene 1. Naturally, you probably want to know what scenes are and how to use them.

There's one catch: *Nobody* uses scenes anymore. Even Adobe recommends that you not use them.

The original idea was that scenes would be a convenient way to organize the Timeline. If you were working with a long movie, you wouldn't have to scroll through thousands of frames; you could just divide the movie into short, manageable scenes. The default, when you opened a new document in Flash, was Scene 1; you then had the option of adding Scene 2, Scene 3, and so on. When you played the movie's SWF file, Flash would concatenate the scenes into a single movie, in numerical order. (If you wanted to, you could even give the scenes descriptive names and rearrange their order; that's what the Scene panel is for.)

There are, however, several drawbacks to using scenes:

- No matter how efficiently you divide your movie into scenes, they still add up to one very long SWF file. Anyone who accesses your movie from the Web has to download that large file, even if they don't intend to watch the whole movie.

- Scenes are confusing in collaborative environments. If you give someone a FLA file to edit, and it's divided into scenes, that person has no way of getting a bird's-eye view of the structure and organization of your movie. Instead of setting the Timeline's cell size to Tiny and seeing most or all of the Timeline at once, the person has to go through the movie scene by scene.

- People tend to write their ActionScript scripts as if the current scene is the entire movie, introducing coding errors that are sometimes difficult to debug. In theory, ActionScript works fine with scenes, but keeping track of scene names and numbers adds an unnecessary level of complexity to scripts.

(continued on next page)

A good alternative to using scenes is to structure your movie as a series of short, individual FLA files. With a line of simple ActionScript, you can instruct each movie to start playing the next one when it ends, so the end result looks the same to the user. But the user gets to download several small SWF files instead of one large one. In fact, you could post individual links to each file in the series, so users need only download the parts of your movie that they want to see.

A collection of FLA files doesn't solve the problem of working in a collaborative environment, where what's in each FLA file is no more apparent than what's in each scene. However, you can have several FLA files open and visible at the same time. With a single FLA file, you can only see one scene at a time.

CHAPTER FIVE

Using Effects and Filters

In the early days of animation, animators used shortcuts to create special effects without having to draw them by hand. For example, the movie camera that photographed the frames of animation could be set to over-expose part of each frame, giving the impression of bright light.

Similarly, Flash has some premade effects that you can use in your movie. These effects come in three types: Timeline Effects, filters, and blending modes. As you'll see in this chapter, each type of effect does things that the others can't, and each has its drawbacks. Knowing how these effects work can open your imagination to ideas that you might not have thought of otherwise.

#45 Applying Timeline Effects

The Timeline Effects feature was originally added to Flash as a way for beginners to do simple animation without having to master the concepts of keyframes and tweening. If you're like most beginners, however, you'll find Timeline Effects to be *less* intuitive than the animation techniques you learned in Chapter 4. Most people use Timeline Effects not as shortcuts to learning Flash, but as tools for creating complex effects more quickly than they could with the standard animation process.

When you apply a Timeline Effect to an object, the object changes its appearance. The change may be instantaneous, or it may take place over time (**Figure 45a**).

Figure 45a This object has had the Transform effect applied to it with a duration of five frames.

Flash offers eight Timeline Effects sorted into three categories.

- **Assistants:** Copy to Grid, Distributed Duplicate
- **Effects:** Blur, Drop Shadow, Expand, Explode
- **Transform/Transition:** Transform, Transition

Figure 45b shows what these effects look like. For more details on each effect, see #46.

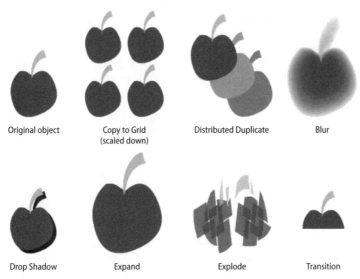

Original object   Copy to Grid (scaled down)   Distributed Duplicate   Blur

Drop Shadow   Expand   Explode   Transition

Figure 45b Typical results of most of the Timeline Effects are illustrated here. (The Transform effect is shown in Figure 45a.)

Here's how you apply a Timeline Effect to an object:

1. Right-click (Windows) or Control-click (Mac) an object on the Stage. The object can be of any type, so long as it isn't tweened and doesn't already have a Timeline Effect applied to it.

2. From the contextual menu, choose Timeline Effects > Category name > Effect name.

(continued on next page)

Flash Within Flash

You may have noticed that the dialog box for Timeline Effects looks different from all the other dialog boxes in Flash. That's because it's not really a dialog box; it's an interactive Flash movie designed to act like a dialog box. It contains some of the same user-interface components that you'll learn about in Chapter 11. Because it's a Flash movie, it looks the same on every computer—unlike ordinary dialog boxes, which vary according to the operating system.

A dialog box appears with a set of controls on the left and a preview pane on the right (**Figure 45c**). The preview pane displays a looping animation showing what the selected object will look like when the Timeline Effect is applied.

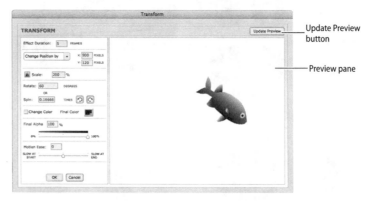

Update Preview button

Preview pane

Figure 45c When you choose a Timeline Effect, you'll see a dialog box similar to this one. The controls on the left differ for each Timeline Effect. (The dialog box shown here is for Transform.)

3. Use the controls to modify the settings for the effect. (See #46 for more information.)

Note that changing a setting doesn't automatically change the animation in the preview pane. To see how your new settings alter the Timeline Effect, click the Update Preview button above the window.

4. Click OK. Several things happen:

- In the Timeline, the selected object is moved to a new layer. The name of the new layer is the chosen Timeline Effect followed by a number—for example, Drop Shadow 1. (If the selected object was on a layer by itself, that layer is renamed.)

- If the Timeline Effect takes place over a number of frames, Flash inserts those frames after the selected object's keyframe. Regardless of whether the Timeline Effect contains animation, it appears in the Timeline as a series of regular frames, not as a tween.

- In the Library, two new symbols appear. The first is a symbol containing your selected object. It's named effectSymbol (followed by a number, if there's more than one), and it's inside the Effects folder. The second is a symbol containing both the effectSymbol and the chosen Timeline Effect. Its name is the Timeline Effect followed by a number.

  The changes to the Library may be slightly different than what's described here, depending on the type of object you selected and the Timeline Effect you chose.

- On the Stage, the selected object appears the way it looked in the Timeline Effect preview pane. If the Timeline Effect you applied takes place over time, you can watch the animation by scrubbing through the Timeline or previewing or testing the movie.

Changing Your Mind

Once you've applied a Timeline Effect to an object, you can edit it by right-clicking (Windows) or Control-clicking (Mac) the object and choosing Timeline Effects > Edit Effect from the contextual menu. Alternatively, you can select the object and click Edit in the Property inspector. Either way, the Timeline Effects dialog box opens and allows you to change any of the effect's settings.

These are the only proper ways to edit a Timeline Effect. Don't go to the Library and edit the symbol labeled Timeline Effect; if you do, you'll no longer be able to change the effect's settings via the dialog box.

You can, however, edit the effectSymbol that contains your selected object; doing so alters the object but not the effect.

To speed up or slow down a Timeline Effect, change the number of frames in the Duration field. Don't try to do this by adding or subtracting frames in the Timeline; if you do, the effect's duration will stay the same, but the effect will either cut out early or begin to loop.

To remove a Timeline Effect from an object, right-click (Windows) or Control-click (Mac) the object and choose Timeline Effects > Remove Effect.

#**46** Modifying Timeline Effects

Whether you're applying a new Timeline Effect or editing one that's already been applied, you'll have to deal with a different set of controls for each effect. Here's a brief description of each effect and some notes about what you'll find in its dialog box:

- **Copy to Grid.** Use this assistant to arrange copies of the selected object in an array. You can specify the number of rows and columns and the spacing between them. This effect is instantaneous; it can't be spread over a series of frames.

- **Distributed Duplicate.** This assistant causes copies of the selected object to extend outward in a straight line. You can specify the number of copies and incrementally transform their spacing, size, color, and opacity. There's no direct way to specify the angle along which the copies are aligned, but you can change the angle indirectly by changing the X and Y values for Offset Distance (**Figure 46a**).

Figure 46a On the left, the Distributed Duplicate effect with default Offset Distance settings of X=25 and Y=25. On the right, the same effect with the X value changed to –25.

You can spread the Distributed Duplicate transition over a series of frames by entering a number in the Offset Start Frame field. The duration of the effect, in frames, is the Offset Start Frame number multiplied by the number of copies.

- **Blur.** This effect causes the selected object's edges to feather gradually. You can specify the amount of the blur (how far the feathered edge extends), the resolution of the blur (how many steps are contained within the feathered edge), and the direction of movement in which the feathered edge extends. Blur is most convincing when applied to an object without any strokes. You can specify the number of frames over which the blurring takes place: The greater the number of frames, the smoother the blur.

Expanding on 'Expand'

The Expand effect does simple things, but it hides them behind an unintuitive interface. With the default settings, the selected object often moves from right to left without expanding, and it continues that unexpected behavior even if you click the arrows on the Direction of Movement control. If you want to change the settings, you're faced with controls named "Shift Group Center by" and "Fragment Offset," which seem to have nothing to do with expanding an object.

The key to using Expand is to understand that it's designed to work with *multiple objects at once*. If you select two or more individual objects—not combined into a group or symbol—and apply the Expand effect, the controls begin to make sense. The collection of objects is treated as a group, and each member of the group is considered a fragment. Text objects behave differently, however: If you select a single text object consisting of two or more characters, each character is treated as a separate fragment.

(continued)

- **Drop Shadow.** As you might expect, this effect gives an object a drop shadow. You can specify the shadow's color, opacity, and offset. The drop shadow is uniform; you can't change its settings over a series of frames.

- **Expand.** Use this effect to make the object gradually increase or decrease in size. You can specify whether you want the object to expand, contract, or alternate between the two to create a pulsing effect. Unlike the other Timeline Effects, Expand can't be applied to editable paths. The settings for this effect are unusually obscure, so they're covered separately in a sidebar called "Expanding on 'Expand.'"

- **Explode.** In this effect an object is broken into fragments that scatter and fade away over the number of frames that you specify (**Figure 46b**). You can specify the direction of the scattering and the distance the fragments travel. (The dialog box refers to the fragments' trajectory as an arc, but it's more of a V-shape.) You can also adjust the fragments' gradual changes in size, orientation, and opacity. It's best to keep the Final Alpha slider at 0 percent: With a higher setting, the fragments fade to the specified opacity by the time they reach the vertex of the V, and if the setting is 50 percent or higher, they fade in again.

Figure 46b This is what the Explode effect looks like. The dashed arrows show the V-shaped path that the fragments follow.

- **Transform.** This effect allows you to transform the selected object's size, position, orientation, color, and opacity, just as you would with an ordinary motion tween. Although the transformation usually takes place over a number of frames, you can make it happen instantaneously by entering 1 in the Effect Duration field.

- **Transition.** This effect causes the selected object to fade or wipe in or out. You can specify the duration and pacing of the transition as well as the direction of the wipe.

Expanding on 'Expand' (continued)

The Fragment Offset control determines how far apart or close together the fragments move. The fragments don't change size unless you enter a new width and height in the "Change Fragment Size by" fields. If you want the entire group to move as a single object, enter numbers in the X and Y fields labeled "Shift Group Center by." Doing so allows you to have two types of movement at once: As the fragments move farther apart or closer together, the collection of fragments changes its position on the Stage.

#47 Applying Filters

Filters, like Timeline Effects, are a way to add special effects to your movie. They're easier to use than Timeline Effects, and they don't add as much to your file size. However, they're less versatile: While Timeline Effects can be applied to nearly every kind of object, filters can be applied only to text and to instances of button and movie-clip symbols.

Flash offers seven filters: Drop Shadow, Blur, Glow, Bevel, Gradient Glow, Gradient Bevel, and Adjust Color. Drop Shadow and Blur are also Timeline Effects. The filter versions of these effects look better and offer more options than the Timeline Effect versions, so use the filters when possible.

To apply a filter:

1. Click the Filters tab at the upper-left corner of the Property inspector to bring up the Filters panel (**Figure 47a**).

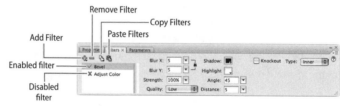

Figure 47a The Filters panel, with controls for the Bevel filter.

2. Select one or more text objects or symbol instances on the Stage. If any are objects that can't have filters applied to them, such as instances of graphic symbols, the Filters panel displays a message telling you so. Change your selection as necessary.

3. Click the Add Filter icon (a plus sign) and choose a filter from the pop-up menu. The selected objects on the Stage show the filter's effects.

4. Use the controls on the Filters panel to modify the settings for the filter. As you do so, the selected objects on the Stage update in real time.

You can add multiple filters to a single object. Each time you add a filter, it appears in the list in the left pane of the Filters panel. To remove a filter, select it and click the Remove Filter icon (a minus sign).

You can temporarily disable a filter without removing it by clicking the green check mark to the left of the filter name. To enable a disabled filter, click the red X.

You can copy filters, along with their settings, from one object to another by using the Copy Filters and Paste Filters icons.

Most of the filter names are self-explanatory. You can see the effects of each filter in **Figure 47b**, and you can learn about their controls in the "Filterpedia" sidebar. The two that you may find unfamiliar are Gradient Glow and Gradient Bevel.

- **Gradient Glow.** This filter is almost identical to the Drop Shadow filter. The only significant difference is that while a drop shadow must be a uniform color, Gradient Glow allows you to make a multicolor shadow.

Filterpedia

Although each filter has different controls, there are some controls that appear more frequently than others.

- **Blur X/Blur Y.** Normally, you'll want the amount of blurring to be the same both horizontally and vertically. To fine-tune the effect, click the lock icon next to the Blur fields, which allows you to set each independently.

- **Strength.** Strength is a combination of darkness and opacity. At 100 percent strength, all filters have some transparency around the edges; if you boost the strength over 100 percent, the transparency begins to disappear.

- **Quality.** The higher the quality setting, the more demands the filter makes on the computer's processor. In most cases, Low is sufficient.

- **Angle.** Three-dimensional effects such as Bevel depend on the illusion of light coming from a particular direction. You can change that direction with the Angle control.

- **Knockout.** Turning on Knockout causes the object to become invisible, leaving only the effect. Since Knockout is either on or off, it can't be tweened (see #48).

- **Outer/Inner.** Outer causes the effect to radiate outward from the edge of the object; Inner causes it to radiate inward. For most filters, the Outer option looks better.

(continued on next page)

You do this by using a gradient slider similar to the one in the Color panel (see #10).

- **Gradient Bevel.** Like the standard Bevel filter, Gradient Bevel gives an object a three-dimensional appearance by adding a highlight to one edge and a shadow to the opposite edge. The difference between them is that Bevel allows you to choose independent colors for the highlight and shadow, while Gradient Bevel requires both colors to be part of a single gradient.

  In the gradient sliders for both of these filters, you'll see a color tab with a gray plus sign on it. This tab can have its color changed, but it can't be moved.

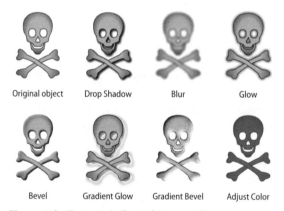

| Original object | Drop Shadow | Blur | Glow |
| Bevel | Gradient Glow | Gradient Bevel | Adjust Color |

Figure 47b The typical effects of the seven filters.

If you like the settings you've made for a particular filter and you think you might want to use them again, you can save them as a preset by choosing Presets > Save As from the Add Filters menu. After you've named the preset and clicked OK, the preset will appear at the bottom of the Presets submenu.

#48 Animating Filters

By default, a filter stays the same as long as an object remains in the Timeline. You can use tweening to animate a filter, allowing it to change over time like a Timeline Effect.

When you apply a filter to an object in any keyframe of a motion tween, Flash applies the same filter in the other keyframes of the tween. (It doesn't keep the settings, however. Numerical controls such as Strength, Distance, and Blur are set to 0.) You can adjust the filter's settings in one keyframe without affecting the other keyframes. Flash tweens the filter's settings in the same way it tweens other characteristics of the object (**Figure 48**).

Figure 48 Flash tweens a filter's settings—in this case, the Glow filter.

Tweening filters can sometimes get messy. When you apply a filter to an object in one keyframe of a tween, Flash doesn't warn you that it's applying that filter in the other keyframes. If you then copy and paste a filter from one keyframe to another, you may end up with multiple copies of the filter in all the keyframes. It's a good idea to check the left pane of the Filters panel now and then to be sure your objects haven't accumulated unnecessary filters.

If you find filters you don't need, cleaning them up is fairly simple. When you remove a filter from an object in one keyframe of a tween, Flash removes the corresponding filters in the other keyframes.

Filters Are a Drag

Although it's tempting to apply filters to objects, keep in mind that filters put heavy demands on the computer that plays back your SWF file. When you animate filters, the load on the processor increases even more. The worst case is when you apply animated filters to animated objects, forcing the computer to do a huge number of calculations to display each frame.

Try these techniques for reducing the performance hit that filters can cause:

- Remove all unnecessary filters and unnecessary tweening of filters. Try to achieve the same effects using standard animation.

- Apply as few filters as possible to any object.

- Set the quality for all your filters to Low.

- If an object has filters applied to it, keep the object still, or confine its movement to a small area of the Stage.

- Avoid applying filters to objects that are rotating or being resized.

#**49** Using Blending Modes

A blending mode isn't a special effect in itself, but rather a tool for creating striking color effects quickly. Many design and animation problems can be solved simply by choosing the right blending mode.

To understand blending modes, consider what happens when you place one object on top of another: If it's opaque, the upper object blocks the view of the lower object. You can apply a blending mode to the top object to reveal all or part of the bottom object (**Figure 49a**).

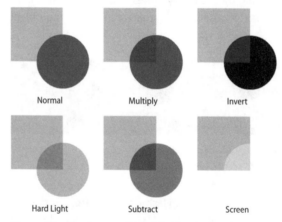

Normal	Multiply	Invert
Hard Light	Subtract	Screen

Figure 49a Here is a sampling of the blending modes available in Flash. Only five are shown; most can't be represented effectively in black and white.

Blending modes are usually described as an interaction between a *blend color* (the one on top) and a *base color* (the one underneath). If the overlapping objects are multicolored, each area of blend color interacts with the base color directly beneath it. Each blending mode is essentially a mathematical formula that determines how the colors interact.

To apply a blending mode, select a movie-clip instance on the Stage, preferably one that has another movie clip partially or totally beneath it. A pop-up menu labeled Blend appears in the lower-right side of the Property inspector (**Figure 49b**). Choosing a blending mode from the menu applies it to the selected object.

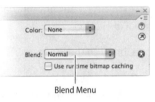

Blend Menu

Figure 49b This menu appears in the Property inspector when a movie-clip instance is selected on the Stage.

Blending modes work equally well whether the two objects are on different layers or are stacked on the same layer. The only limitation is that both objects *must* be instances of movie clips; if they're not, the Property inspector won't display the Blend menu. If you want to blend a different kind of object—text, for example—convert it to a movie clip.

Each blending mode has a technical description that you can read in Flash Help. However, only the most technically minded people find these descriptions useful in predicting what a blend will look like. Instead, when a blend is needed, most people try out all of the blending modes and see what happens. As you get more experienced, you'll know which modes are most likely to be useful for a particular pair of objects.

The Alpha and Erase blending modes deserve special attention because they're designed especially for masking. The masking feature in Flash (see #41) is limited to masks with hard edges, but the Alpha and Erase blending modes allow you to make masks with soft edges.

(continued on next page)

Color by Numbers

Many of the blending-mode formulas require colors to be added, subtracted, or multiplied. The Multiply blending mode, for example, "multiplies the blend color by the base color" according to Flash Help. But how is it possible to do math with colors?

Remember that every color on your computer is made up of three primary colors: red, green, and blue. The amount of each primary color can be specified as a percentage, with 100% representing the maximum amount of that color. Pea green, for example, is a mix of 50% red, 75% green, and 25% blue.

When Flash calculates blends, it does simple arithmetic with each primary color. For example, if pea green above is multiplied by neutral gray (50% red, 50% green, and 50% blue), Flash would calculate 50% $\times$ 50% = 25% for red, 75% $\times$ 50% = 37.5% for green, and 50% $\times$ 25% = 12.5% for blue, yielding a color that's half as bright as the original.

The symbol names here are just suggestions; you can call them whatever you want.

1. Create a movie-clip symbol containing anything at all—for example, animation, a drawing, a bitmap, or text. This is the content that's going to be masked, so name the symbol *m_masked*.

2. Drag an instance of *m_masked* from the Library to the Stage.

3. Select the instance of *m_masked* and choose Modify > Convert to Symbol. (Obviously *m_masked* is already a symbol, but this step nests the instance inside a new symbol.) In the Convert to Symbol dialog box, click the Movie Clip radio button, name the symbol *m_sandwich*, and click OK.

4. Double-click *m_sandwich* in the Library to put it into editing mode. The symbol's Timeline should have one layer and one keyframe containing an instance of *m_masked*. Lock the layer.

5. Add a new layer above the existing layer on *m_sandwich's* Timeline. Flash inserts a blank keyframe.

6. With the blank keyframe selected, use the Rectangle tool to make a rectangle slightly larger than the content in *m_masked*. Fill the rectangle with the standard black-and-white radial gradient (the one that appears on all of the color menus in Flash). The filled rectangle will cover up the instance of *m_masked*, but that's okay.

7. Select the rectangle's fill. The radial gradient is now available for editing in the Color panel.

8. Click the white color tab on the gradient slider in the Color panel.

9. Just above the gradient slider is an Alpha control set to 100 percent. Use the slider or type in a value to bring Alpha down to 0 percent.

10. Deselect the rectangle on the Stage. You can now see *m_masked* through the transparent portion of the gradient.

11. Using the gradient slider and/or the Gradient Transform tool, modify the gradient so that it neatly frames *m_masked* (**Figure 49c**).

Gradient used as a mask (*m_mask*) ⎯⎯⎯⎯

Masked content (*m_masked*) ⎯⎯⎯

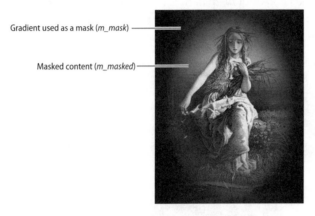

Figure 49c The movie clip *m_mask*, on the top layer, frames the content in *m_masked*, on the bottom layer.

12. Deselect the rectangle on the Stage. You can now see *m_masked* through the white portion of the gradient.

13. Reselect the rectangle and choose Modify > Convert to Symbol to convert it to a movie clip. Name the movie clip *m_mask*.

14. The rectangle (now an instance of *m_mask*) should still be selected. From the Blend menu in the Property inspector, choose Erase.

The mask disappears temporarily, but that's OK. The Erase blending mode has invisibly "erased" the areas of *m_masked* that are covered by the more opaque portions of the mask.

15. Click Scene 1 on the breadcrumb trail to return to the main Timeline. The instance of *m_sandwich* should still be on the Stage.

(continued on next page)

16. Select the instance of *m_sandwich* if it's not already selected. From the Blend menu in the Property inspector, choose Layer.

The content of *m_masked* is now framed by a soft-edged mask. If you wish, you can put some sort of background behind it to complete the effect (**Figure 49d**).

Figure 49d A cloud-filled background completes the effect. The Layer blending mode applied to *m_sandwich* allows the background to show through.

CHAPTER SIX

Importing Artwork

Flash has a versatile set of drawing tools, but they may not always be enough to meet your needs. Perhaps you're not very good at drawing from scratch, and you find it helpful to bring in outside images and trace them. Perhaps you prefer the tools in Fireworks or Illustrator and want to create your drawings in those programs. Perhaps you want to use bit-mapped images such as photographs or scanned artwork.

These are some of the reasons that Flash lets you import artwork in a variety of vector and bitmap formats. In many cases, you can even modify the artwork in Flash. Thanks to the program's ever-expanding import capabilities, you can be an animator without drawing a single stroke.

#50 Taking Advantage of Creative Suite Integration

Before you can import artwork, you first have to figure out what you want to import. You may need to sort through hundreds of files on your hard drive, preview them in Photoshop or Illustrator, rate their suitability, and gather together the ones you decide to use.

Doing these things has become easier now that Flash is part of Adobe Creative Suite. In the File menu you'll see a new command called Browse. Choosing this command brings up an attractive, flexible, easy-to-use file manager/viewer (**Figure 50a**). This new file-management tool, called Bridge, isn't part of Flash; it's a separate program that's accessible from the File menu in nearly every Creative Suite application. Bridge is the glue that ties the suite together.

Preview

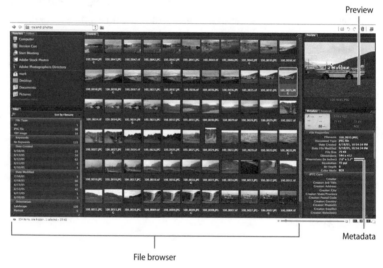

File browser

Metadata

Figure 50a This is the default Bridge workspace. Like the Flash workspace, it can be reconfigured in different ways for different purposes.

A separate book could be written just on using Bridge. (In fact, several have been.) Instead of trying to describe everything it can do, we'll just mention the simplest features—the ones you can use right away:

- You can navigate to any folder on your computer or network and see thumbnails of nearly all the visual content—not just bitmapped images and vector drawings, but even video files and PDFs.

- You can select any of the thumbnails and see what's inside it without opening the file. A preview panel at the upper-right corner of the Bridge window lets you view artwork and even watch movies and animation. (The viewer doesn't support FLA files, but it can preview SWF files.)

- A Metadata panel below the viewer gives you information about the selected file, including its name, type, creation date, and size. Depending on the type of file and where it came from, there may be other information as well, such as who took a photo and what kind of camera it was taken with.

- If you find a file that you want to import into Flash, you can drag it from the Bridge window directly onto the Flash Stage. The appropriate Import dialog box appears, just as if you had chosen File > Import from the menu (see #51).

Creative Suite includes another "meta-application" besides Bridge: Version Cue, a workflow manager designed for multiuser environments. It ensures, for example, that if one person is editing a FLA file, nobody else can edit the same file at the same time. Setting up and maintaining a Version Cue server is usually the job of computer professionals, which puts it outside the scope of this book.

When you begin to import files, you'll see that membership in Creative Suite has given Flash another benefit: Adobe has begun to integrate Flash with Illustrator and Photoshop, making it possible to move artwork from one program to another with minimal loss of information or functionality. (Import options for those programs are covered in #51 and #52.) The eventual goal is to make Flash, Photoshop, Bridge, and the other members of Creative Suite seem as if they're all parts of a single program.

#51 Importing from Adobe Illustrator

Although the drawing tools in Flash are easy for beginners to learn, many experienced artists and designers prefer to create their vector drawings in Illustrator. Now that Adobe has bundled Flash and Illustrator in the Creative Suite, using the two programs together is easier than it's ever been.

The usual ways to bring Illustrator artwork into Flash are to copy and paste directly from Illustrator, or to save it in Adobe Illustrator (AI) format and import it into Flash.

Let's look at the copy-and-paste technique first. You can select individual objects or entire layers from an Illustrator document and choose Edit > Copy to copy the selection to the computer's clipboard; then switch to Flash and choose Edit > Paste in Place or Edit > Paste in Center. A dialog box appears with the following options:

- **Paste as bitmap.** This option causes all the copied material to be pasted into Flash as a single bitmapped image. This is the simplest option; it places only one object on the Stage and one item in the Library. However, pasting as a bitmap means losing all the advantages of vector objects—for example, you can no longer reshape paths or select individual anchor points.

- **Paste using AI File Importer preferences.** This option preserves most of the attributes of the copied artwork. Editable paths and text remain editable; Illustrator symbols become Flash symbols; masks remain masks. You can go to Edit > Preferences (Windows) or Flash > Preferences (Mac) and select AI File Importer to determine how Flash handles specific types of objects—for example, whether text objects are imported as editable text or vector paths.

  The remaining two options are available only if you've chosen "Paste using AI File Importer preferences."

- **Apply recommended import settings to resolve incompatibilities.** This option determines how Flash handles objects with attributes that it doesn't support, such as Illustrator's Distort & Transform or 3D effects. If you choose this option, Flash converts these objects as simply as possible to bitmaps or groups of drawing objects. If you don't choose this option, Flash maintains the editability of the imported objects by converting them to complex, multilayered symbols. Either way, the objects maintain the same appearance that they had in Illustrator (**Figure 51a**).

Figure 51a On the left, a simple path in Illustrator with the 3D effect applied. In the center, the same path pasted into Flash using the "Apply recommended import settings…" option; it's been converted to a bitmap. On the right, the path pasted *without* using that option; it's become a group of subgroups nested within more subgroups.

- **Maintain layers.** If the artwork you're pasting has multiple layers, choosing this option preserves those layers in Flash. The drawback is that Flash does this by ignoring the layers and keyframes already in the Timeline: No matter what keyframe is selected at the time you paste, Flash creates new layers and pastes the artwork into frame 1. If you don't choose this option, your pasted artwork comes in on a single layer, but you can paste it into any keyframe on any existing layer.

The other technique is to save your Illustrator artwork as an AI file and import the file into Flash. This technique gives you more control than you get with copying and pasting.

In Flash, choose File > Import > Import to Stage and navigate to the AI file that you want to import. When you click Open (Windows) or Import (Mac), a large Import to Stage dialog box appears.

The left pane shows a hierarchical list of every layer and sublayer in the AI file. Each is accompanied by a check box that indicates whether it will be imported to Flash. All the check boxes are initially selected, but you can deselect them for layers or sublayers that you want to exclude.

When you click any item in the left pane, the right pane offers a list of possible import options for that item. Each has an option already selected; if you don't want to look at every item, you can accept those default choices. In most cases, the items you'll want to look at are those that have a warning icon (an exclamation mark in a yellow triangle) to

(continued on next page)

their right. The icon indicates that the layer or sublayer contains features that Flash doesn't support (**Figure 51b**). To see a list of those problem items, click the Incompatibility Report button below the left pane.

Warning icon

Recommended import option

Figure 51b This is the upper portion of the Import to Stage dialog box. An incompatible item is selected in the left pane; the right pane shows the recommended import option.

The bottom area of the dialog box provides a series of options:

- **Convert layers to.** This menu offers three choices. Two of them, Flash Layers and Single Flash Layer, do the same things as "Maintain layers" in the Paste dialog box. The third choice, Keyframes, converts Illustrator layers to a series of keyframes in a Flash layer.

Tip
If you don't like the drawing tools in Flash, you can do frame-by-frame animation in Illustrator. Draw each frame on a separate layer, then import the AI file to Flash by selecting Keyframes in the "Convert layers to" menu. In Flash, you can refine the animation and add tweens.

- **Place objects at original position.** This option causes the location of the imported artwork to have the same relationship to the Flash Stage as it had to the Illustrator artboard. (It's similar to choosing Edit > Paste in Place as opposed to Edit > Paste in Center.)

- **Set Stage size to same size as Illustrator artboard.** This option is self-explanatory.

- **Import unused symbols.** Use this option to put all of the symbols from the Illustrator Symbols panel into the Flash Library, regardless of whether they've been used on Illustrator's artboard.

- **Import as a single bitmap image.** This option is the same as the "Paste as bitmap" option in the Paste dialog box.

Directly below Import to Stage in the Edit > Import submenu is the Import to Library option. It does the same things as Import to Stage, except that it doesn't place the imported artwork on the Stage or in the Timeline. Instead, it creates a symbol in the Library with the same name as the AI file and puts the imported artwork inside it.

Tip
Another way to import an AI file (or any file) is to drag it directly onto the Flash Stage from a folder or your computer's desktop. The Import to Stage dialog box appears just as if you had chosen File > Import > Import to Stage.

#52 Importing from Adobe Photoshop

Importing Photoshop (PSD) files to Flash used to be a one-step process with no options: Everything in a PSD file was converted to a single-layer bitmap. Now that Flash and Photoshop are Creative Suite members, that's no longer the case. Although Flash doesn't edit bitmaps very well, it can identify some of the non-bitmapped elements of a PSD file and keep them editable.

Choose Edit > Preferences (Windows) or Flash > Preferences (Mac) and click the PSD File Importer category. (These preference settings, along with those for the AI File Importer, are new to Flash.) Although the default settings are to import Photoshop files as bitmaps, you'll see that there are now options to preserve the editability of layer styles, text, and vector paths (**Figure 52a**).

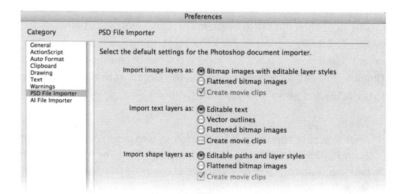

Figure 52a If you want to preserve the editability of the non-bitmapped parts of a PSD file, use these preference settings instead of the defaults.

These new import capabilities are not quite as comprehensive as they seem. When Flash refers to "layer styles," it really means *blending modes*. Real Photoshop layer styles (such as Drop Shadow and Outer Glow) are flattened into bitmaps when imported to Flash. Even text and vector paths—which normally remain editable after import—are rasterized in Flash if layer styles have been applied to them in Photoshop.

On the positive side, Flash recognizes and preserves Photoshop layers and layer groups (formerly called *layer sets*). It also preserves transparency in PSD files (**Figure 52b**).

Figure 52b Anything that appears against a gray-and-white checkerboard in Photoshop (left) will have a transparent background when imported into Flash (right).

The procedure for importing PSD files is the same as that for importing AI files (see #51). When you choose File > Import > Import to Stage and navigate to a PSD file, Flash opens an Import to Stage dialog box with a list of layers, allowing you to choose an import option for each layer. (These individual import options can override the ones you set in Preferences.)

One significant difference from importing AI files is the ability to merge layers when importing PSD files. In the Import to Stage dialog box, you can select multiple layers by clicking the first layer and Command-clicking (Windows) or Control-clicking (Mac) additional layers. When two or more layers have been selected, a Merge Layers button becomes available below the left pane. Clicking that button causes the selected layers to become dimmed and a specialized layer labeled Merged Bitmap to take their place. If you change your mind, you can select the Merged Bitmap layer and click the Merge Layers button (which is now labeled Separate).

It's possible to copy and paste from Photoshop directly into Flash, but with severe limitations. Copying and pasting works only with bitmaps, not with vector paths or text. Flash doesn't recognize transparency, layers, blending modes, or other non-bitmap elements when you copy and paste.

#53 Importing from Adobe Fireworks

The Thing About PNG

PNG (which stands for Portable Network Graphics and is usually pronounced *ping*) was originally intended to replace GIF and JPEG as the standard file format for the Web. Although that goal was never realized, the developers of Fireworks adopted PNG as the program's native format.

Although other programs can also save to the PNG format, most don't take full advantage of its features. A PNG file created by Fireworks may contain bitmaps, vectors, editable text, layer information, and so on. A PNG file created by most other programs—including Photoshop—is often just a flattened bitmap.

Because they're both former Macromedia products, Flash has a much closer relationship with Fireworks than it has with Illustrator or Photoshop. In many ways, Flash and Fireworks behave as if they're a single program.

Unlike Photoshop and Illustrator files, Fireworks files can contain multiple frames (for animation) or multiple pages (for Web publishing). Both of these features are preserved in Flash. In fact, copying and pasting from Fireworks to Flash preserves nearly all attributes of the pasted artwork; so does importing a Fireworks PNG file into Flash. In either case, an Import Fireworks Document dialog box with a few simple options appears:

- **Import as a single flattened bitmap.** Any aspects of the artwork that would otherwise have been editable in Flash—such as layers, text, and vector paths—are reduced to pixels. If the file contains multiple frames or pages, only the first is imported. Choosing this option causes the others in the dialog box to become unavailable.

- **Import [Page #].** This option allows you to choose which page of a multipage file you want to import. You can choose a single page or all pages. If you import all pages, each page comes in as a separate movie clip.

- **Into.** This option lets you specify whether the imported artwork will be placed in the currently selected keyframe or whether Flash will create a new layer for it. This option is similar to the "Maintain layers" option in the Paste AI to Stage dialog box (see #51).

- **Objects.** This option provides two choices: "Import as bitmaps to maintain appearance" has the same effect as "Import as a single flattened bitmap" (above), except that layers from the Fireworks file are preserved. "Keep all paths [or text] editable" preserves full editability.

- **Text.** This option has the same choices as Objects.

If you want to edit imported AI or PSD files, you have to return to Illustrator or Photoshop to edit the artwork there, and then reimport it to Flash. With Fireworks PNG files, that's not always necessary. Here's the easiest method for round-trip editing between Flash and Fireworks:

1. Import a Fireworks PNG file to Flash by choosing File > Import > Import to Stage, or by dragging the PNG file icon onto the Stage.

2. In the Import to Stage dialog box, choose "Import as a single flattened bitmap." This option makes the artwork uneditable in Flash, but that's OK—you'll be doing your editing in Fireworks.

3. When you're ready to edit the Fireworks artwork, select it on the Stage. An Edit button appears in the Property inspector (**Figure 53a**).

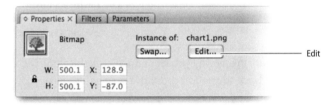

Figure 53a When you select a Fireworks bitmap on the Stage, this button appears in the Property inspector.

Keeping the Fire in Fireworks

Before the Adobe/Macromedia merger, one way that Macromedia competed against Adobe's more-extensive image editing programs was by integrating Fireworks tightly with Flash and Dreamweaver. A single click in either program sends an image to Fireworks for editing; another click brings the edited image back. The ease of this round-trip editing feature led many designers to use Fireworks when they would otherwise have used an Adobe program.

When Flash and Dreamweaver became part of Adobe Creative Suite, it seemed unlikely that Fireworks would survive. Why would anyone use Fireworks when they could just as conveniently use Photoshop or Illustrator? Fireworks has remained in the suite, perhaps because Flash still can't do round-trip editing with Photoshop and Illustrator. (If so, when that limitation is overcome, Fireworks might indeed disappear.) But it's also possible that Adobe intends to give Fireworks a more prominent role, making it as indispensable for Web-related image formats as Illustrator is for vector drawings and Photoshop is for bitmaps. Adobe has already moved in that direction, giving Fireworks new features—such as the ability to store multiple pages in a single file—that Photoshop and Illustrator lack.

(continued on next page)

Side Trip

When you've selected a Fireworks bitmap on the Stage,
sometimes the Edit button
in the Property inspector is
dimmed. This means that
Flash has lost track of the
original PNG file from which
you imported the artwork. To
fix the problem, you'll have to
take a slight detour from the
round-trip editing process:

1. Check the Property
   inspector for the name
   of the selected bitmap;
   then locate that bitmap
   in the Library.

2. Double-click the Bit-
   map icon (a tiny tree) to
   the left of the bitmap's
   name. A Bitmap Proper-
   ties dialog box appears.

3. Click the Import button.
   An Import Bitmap
   window appears.

4. Navigate to your PNG file
   and click Open.

5. Click OK to close the Bitmap Properties dialog
   box. The bitmap on the
   Stage remains selected,
   and the Edit button
   should now be available
   in the Property inspector.

4. Click the Edit button. Fireworks launches, if it's not already running. The PNG file corresponding to the imported bitmap opens in Fire-works. (See "Side Trip" for more information about this step.)

Near the top of the Fireworks editing window, you'll see an Editing from Flash icon and a Done button (**Figure 53b**).

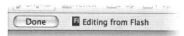

Figure 53b This bar appears in the Fireworks editing window when round-trip editing from Flash is in process.

5. Modify the artwork in any way you want, then click the Done button.

Flash comes back to the foreground. Your revised version of the bitmapped artwork has replaced the previous version on the Stage. Behind the scenes, Fireworks automatically saves the revised PNG file.

#54 Importing from Other Sources

Although the Import feature in Flash is geared primarily for Illustrator, Photoshop, and Fireworks, Flash can import several other formats, including:

- **DXF.** This vector file format is used by AutoCAD and other computer-aided drawing applications. Flash imports DXF files that fit a narrow set of criteria: They must be coded in ASCII rather than binary; they must be 2D rather than 3D; and they must use the AutoCAD 10 file format. Once imported into Flash, DXF files are fully editable.

- **FH7 through FH11.** Although Adobe has stopped developing and marketing FreeHand (which competed with Illustrator), it still includes support for FH files in Flash. When you import an FH file, Flash opens a FreeHand Import dialog box (**Figure 54a**). All FreeHand features are preserved when the file is imported.

Figure 54a Although the options in the FreeHand Import dialog box are worded slightly differently, they function almost identically to those in the dialog boxes for AI and Fireworks imports.

- **BMP, GIF, JPEG, PNG.** Flash imports these common bitmap file formats, but without offering any import options. The Import to Stage dialog box doesn't appear, and the PSD and AI File Importer preferences don't apply.

- **TIFF, TGA.** Flash doesn't import files in these formats directly, but if QuickTime 4 or later is installed on your computer (as it is on all Macs and many PCs), Flash will use it as a translator for these and a few more obscure formats. You don't have to do anything special; Flash handles the QuickTime translation behind the scenes.

Flash Is Not Your Mother

Flash can do a lot with imported artwork—scale it, change its color mode, merge layers, and so on—but Flash shouldn't have to do these tasks. You should take responsibility for preparing your files *before* you import them into Flash.

- **Color mode.** Flash uses the RGB color mode exclusively. If you import a CMYK, grayscale, or indexed-color file, Flash silently converts it to RGB. But for the best results, you should convert the files to RGB yourself. Flash does a satisfactory job of conversion, but Photoshop and Illustrator do it better. Those programs also give you a chance to tweak the color.

- **Scaling.** Flash lets you import huge bitmaps and scale them down on the Stage, but there's no good reason to do that. Importing more pixels than will be seen in your movie makes the FLA file unwieldy, bloats the SWF file, and slows down your movie.

- **Layers.** Unless you plan to do round-trip editing in Fireworks, there's no need to have Flash flatten your bitmaps. Do it yourself in Photoshop.

#55 Setting Bitmap Properties

Bringing a bitmap into Flash is easy, but using the bitmap effectively is more difficult. Unlike vector drawings, bitmaps suffer a loss in quality every time they're scaled or rotated. In addition, bitmap files tend to contain more information than equivalent vector-based files, which makes them less suitable for animation. Adding bitmaps to a movie can significantly increase the size of the SWF file and put a heavy load on the computer's processor.

You can minimize these problems by fine-tuning each bitmap's properties. Select a bitmap in the Library and either double-click its icon or click the Properties icon at the bottom of the Library panel (see #29). Either way, the Bitmap Properties dialog box appears (**Figure 55a**).

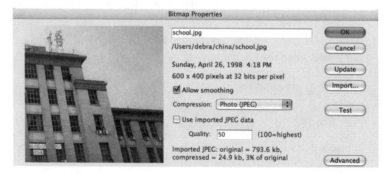

Figure 55a The Bitmap Properties dialog box is where you change the smoothing setting and compression options for each imported bitmap.

If the bitmap looks rough or ragged when it's been resized or rotated on the Stage, you can select the "Allow smoothing" check box. Nearly every bitmap—except, perhaps, for very small ones—looks better with smoothing applied. The trade-off is that animating a smoothed bitmap requires more work from the processor than animating an unsmoothed bitmap, so it's possible that the playback performance of your movie will suffer.

An unwieldy bitmap file size can be dealt with by applying compression. Flash lets you choose between two types: lossless and photo, which is more commonly known as JPEG compression. Lossless compression squeezes the file's information into a smaller space with no loss in quality. It's effective on bitmaps that have large areas of flat color, such as diagrams or cartoons. For images that have many colors or gradients, such as paintings or photographs, JPEG compression is more effective. It shrinks the file size by deleting nonessential information.

JPEG compression is the type you'll probably use most frequently. JPEG offers varying degrees of image quality, on a scale from 0 to 100. As image quality increases, so does file size. Your challenge is to find the ideal quality setting for each bitmap: the point on the scale at which the file size is as small as it can be without a significant sacrifice of image quality. There's no right or wrong quality level; it's entirely a matter of judgment.

Here's how you set the JPEG compression level:

1. In the Bitmap Properties dialog box, choose Photo (JPEG) from the Compression menu.

2. If the imported bitmap has a .jpg or .jpeg file extension, it's already compressed. If you're satisfied with the level of compression, skip to step 6. Otherwise, deselect the "Use imported JPEG data" or the "Use document default quality" check box. A Quality field appears with a default setting of 50.

3. Type a different number into the Quality field. Click the Test button to try out the setting.

4. Look at the preview pane on the left side of the dialog box to see what effect the quality setting has on the bitmap. If you see blocky or muddy areas, the quality is too low (**Figure 55b**).

Figure 55b An optimal level of JPEG compression (left) may include some minor flaws, such as a bit of fuzziness around sharp edges. If you see obvious blockiness or muddiness (right), the compression level is too high.

Look also at the text at the bottom of the dialog box. It shows you the original file size, the compressed file size, and their relationship expressed as a percentage. In most cases, if the compressed file size is more than 5 percent of the original, the quality is too high.

5. Repeat steps 3 and 4 as many times as necessary to find the best balance of quality and file size.

6. Click OK to close the Bitmap Properties dialog box.

#56 Breaking Apart Bitmaps

Flash treats bitmaps much like it does symbols. Once a bitmap is in the Library, you can drag as many instances as you like to the Stage, and you can motion-tween those instances just as you would instances of symbols.

In some cases, you may want to convert bitmaps to symbols. For example, if you want to apply a blending mode to a bitmap, you have to turn it into a movie clip first.

In other cases, however, you may want to do the opposite: Make a bitmap behave more like an editable path than like a symbol. To do this, select the bitmap on the Stage and choose Edit > Break Apart.

Breaking apart a bitmap allows you to do two things to it that you couldn't do otherwise: You can select portions of the bitmap, and you can turn the bitmap into a fill for a path.

- **Selecting.** If you've used Photoshop or similar programs, you know that you can use a variety of tools to select different portions of a bitmap. The same is possible in Flash, albeit on a more primitive level. You can use the Selection tool to select rectangular areas (**Figure 56a**), or the Lasso tool to select irregular areas.

Figure 56a By drawing a marquee with the Selection tool, you can select a rectangular portion of a broken-apart bitmap. (Flash highlights the selected area with a dot screen.)

Flash even has an equivalent to Photoshop's Magic Wand tool. If you select the Lasso tool and look at the options area at the bottom of the toolbar, you'll see a Magic Wand icon. Directly below it is the Magic Wand Settings icon, which opens a dialog box in which you can set the wand's tolerance. The Magic Wand allows you to select contiguous areas of similar color with a single click (**Figure 56b**).

Figure 56b Clicking a black pixel with the Magic Wand causes that and all contiguous black pixels to be selected.

Once you've selected a portion of a bitmap, you can move, transform, delete, or change the color of the selected area.

- **Converting to a fill.** If you click a broken-apart bitmap with the Eyedropper tool, a tiny thumbnail of the bitmap appears in the Fill Color control. Any path you create at that point will be filled not with a color or a gradient, but with an instance of the bitmap (**Figure 56c**).

Tip
To scale, rotate, or skew a bitmap fill, or to change its position in relation to the filled object, use the Gradient Transform Tool (see #10).

Figure 56c The Paintbrush tool, which can make only fills, is being used here to "paint" a new instance of the bitmap.

Abracadabra

The Magic Wand is one of the most time-saving tools you can use with bitmaps. You can select an entire irregularly shaped area by clicking the Magic Wand inside it, provided that all the pixels in that area are approximately the same color.

You can control the sensitivity of the Magic Wand by clicking the Magic Wand Settings icon and entering a value in the Threshold field. The higher the Threshold setting, the more tolerant the Magic Wand is. For example, with a Threshold setting of 0, the Magic Wand selects only pixels that are exactly the same color as the pixel you click. With a Threshold setting of 36, the Magic Wand accepts pixels that aren't quite the same color, as long as they're not more than 36 shades away from the color of the first pixel. With a Threshold setting of 200 (the maximum), clicking the Magic Wand anywhere in the bitmap selects nearly every pixel.

#57 Autotracing Bitmaps

Given the drawbacks of bitmaps in Flash—large file sizes, poor scalability, and limited editability—it might seem like a good idea to convert your bitmaps to vector drawings. Doing this, however, is not as straightforward as it sounds. In real life, there are no outlines: Photographs typically contain soft-edged shapes, blurriness, noise, and subtle gradations of color.

Originally, the only way to "vectorize" a bitmapped image was to trace it by hand, figuring out where each new outline should go. Since then, some programs have automated the process: The software guesses where the edges are by looking for boundaries between differently colored groups of pixels, then it draws paths along those edges. This process is generally known as *autotracing*.

The autotracing feature built into Flash is good, but it's far from perfect. A bitmapped image—especially a photograph—that's been converted to vectors never looks like the original image, but more like an Andy Warhol silkscreen (**Figure 57a**). Still, in some cases, that may be the look you want.

Figure 57a The original photograph (left) is autotraced with a low color threshold (center) and a high color threshold (right).

To convert a bitmap to a vector drawing, select it on the Stage and choose Modify > Bitmap > Trace Bitmap. A Trace Bitmap dialog box appears, containing four settings for you to specify.

- **Color Threshold.** This should be a number between 1 and 500. A low number produces an image with lots of color variation and a large file size; a high number produces an image with fewer colors, a posterized appearance, and a smaller file size.

- **Minimum Area.** This number should be between 1 and 1000. This is the number of pixels that Flash looks at to determine the average color of an area. A low number produces a more detailed image with a large file size; a high number produces a "blobbier" image with a smaller file size.

- **Curve Fit.** This setting determines how Flash will draw outlines. The tightest fit (Pixels) results in a very precise, detailed image, but the file size may be greater than that of the original bitmap. The loosest fit (Very Smooth) yields an image that looks like it was drawn in a moving car, but its file size is much smaller.

- **Corner Threshold.** This setting determines the degree to which jagged outlines will be smoothed. Choosing the Many Corners option produces a sharper image with a larger file size; choosing Few Corners produces a softer image with a smaller file size.

As with compression, there's no hard-and-fast formula for determining the proper settings. Every image is different, and you have to experiment with different combinations of settings to see what works best in each case.

This process of trial and error has become much easier now that a Preview button has been added to the Trace Bitmap dialog box. Each time you change the settings, you can click Preview to see what the autotraced image will look like on the Stage.

CHAPTER SEVEN

Working with Sound

Animation and sound go together like pie and ice cream. No matter how appealing your animation is, it won't engage your audience nearly as well unless you back it up with appropriate music and add some well-chosen sound effects.

Flash can't create or record sound, and its sound-editing ability is minimal. If you want to add music or other sounds to a Flash movie, you either have to record it yourself or use prerecorded sounds from CDs or the Web. Either way, you'll almost always want to use a sound-editing program to adjust the length, volume, and quality of the sound. The cost of sound-editing software ranges from free (Audacity, an open-source program downloadable from www.sourceforge.net) to thousands of dollars (Digidesign's Pro Tools, the choice of most audio professionals). A good intermediate choice is Adobe Soundbooth, a new member of the Creative Suite that can export files compatible with ActionScript.

Once you've imported your sound files, Flash takes care of the rest. You can play multiple audio tracks at once, synchronize sound to animation in a variety of ways, and even apply effects such as fades and pans. Best of all, you can do these things using the techniques you're already familiar with: inserting keyframes, setting compression levels, and using the Property inspector to modify instances.

#58 Importing Audio Files

To import a sound file, choose File > Import > Import to Library, navigate to the file you want to import, and click Open (Windows) or Import to Library (Mac). There are no options and no dialog boxes; the file appears immediately in the Library. If you select the filename in the Library, you see a visual representation of the sound—called a *waveform*—in the viewing pane (**Figure 58a**). To hear the sound, click the Play button above the waveform.

Note
Choosing Import to Stage instead of Import to Library makes no difference. Either way, the audio file is imported to the Library. (Since a sound isn't visible, it can't appear on the Stage.)

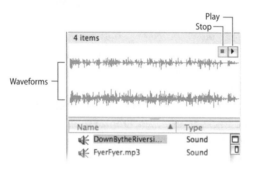

Figure 58a Because this is a stereo sound file, two waveforms display in the Library's viewing pane. For a mono sound, only one waveform would appear.

On its own, Flash can import only three audio file formats: WAV (Windows), AIFF (Mac), and MP3 (both platforms). If your computer has QuickTime installed, Flash can import WAV and AIFF on both platforms, along with a few other specialized formats such as Sun AU.

Of the audio formats that Flash imports, only MP3 is compressed: It uses a combination of lossless and "lossy" compression (see #55) to squeeze high-quality audio into a relatively small file. If a particular sound is available in a variety of formats, it's generally best to import one of the uncompressed formats (such as WAV or AIFF) because for uncompressed sounds, Flash does its own compression when it generates a SWF file. If a sound is already compressed, Flash leaves it alone. The compression that Flash performs is usually preferable because it's optimized for Flash Player.

Like bitmaps, sounds add considerably to the size of the SWF file. Although the sound compression in Flash works well, it's even more effective if you have a smaller file to begin with. Here are suggestions for using your sound-editing software to prepare files for Flash:

- Convert stereo sounds to mono. Because it contains two audio channels, a stereo file is twice the size of an equivalent mono file.

- Downsample your sounds to the lowest acceptable sampling rate. Music usually doesn't sound good at rates below 22 kHz, but sound effects can often be brought down to 11 kHz with adequate quality.

- Save your sounds at a lower bit rate. You'll probably want a 16-bit file for most music, but 8 bits is usually sufficient for speech and sound effects.

- Edit out unneeded parts of sound files. If you're experienced at sound editing, you may be able to extract part of an instrumental track and edit it to loop seamlessly, which gives you a much smaller file than using the whole track—and most of your audience won't notice. At least trim off the few seconds of silence at the beginning and end of many music tracks.

Copyright: This Is Serious

Whenever you import assets that were created outside of Flash—drawings, photographs, sound, or video—you have to pay attention to copyright laws. The basic rule is simple: Unless the imported item is something you created yourself, you can't use it in your Flash movie without permission. The recording industry and Hollywood movie studios have become especially vigilant about stopping misuse of their material, even to the point of suing individuals like you for thousands of dollars.

There are plenty of myths about copyright: that it's OK to use copyrighted work if you're not making any money from it, or if you use less than 10 seconds of it, or if you make minor changes in it. None of these are true. The only legal way to include someone else's work in your Flash movie is if you have written permission from the creator or owner of that work. The copyright owner may require you to do something in exchange for that permission, such as pay a fee.

If you don't want to deal with copyright owners directly, there are more convenient solutions. All over the Web, you'll find stock photo or music sites that streamline the permissions process by letting you download material (and granting you the license to use it) in exchange for paying a fee. Some of these sites let you use the material at no charge if it's for personal or educational purposes. In online communities such as http://flashkit.com, Flash users share their own animation and music loops with others. Finally, you can purchase "buy-out CDs," for which the price includes permission to reuse the CD's music or video files.

#59 Comparing Event Sounds with Streaming Sounds

Flash divides sounds into event sounds and streaming sounds. The difference isn't inherent in the sounds themselves; you can use any sound file either as an event sound or a streaming sound. The difference is in how Flash Player handles them when it plays a SWF file.

When you open a Flash movie in a Web browser, Flash Player *streams* the movie: It downloads just enough of the SWF file to begin playing it, and then continues to download the file while the movie plays. All the elements of the movie—paths, bitmaps, text, sounds, video, and so on—download in the order they appear in the Timeline.

Because sounds tend to have large file sizes, they're sometimes not fully downloaded by the time the playhead reaches them in the Timeline. Event sounds and streaming sounds behave differently in this situation.

If an event sound is still downloading at the time it's needed in the movie, the movie pauses to let the download continue and then resumes when the sound file has downloaded completely. If a streaming sound isn't fully downloaded, it begins to play and continues to download behind the scenes, just as the full SWF file does. Therefore, a general rule is that short, fast-downloading sound files work better as event sounds, while longer sound files work better as streaming sounds.

An exception to that rule applies to looping sounds. Any sound that's intended to loop—that is, to play multiple times in a row—should be designated as an event sound regardless of how long or short it is. That's because no matter how many times it plays in a movie, an event sound downloads only once. If you were to loop a streaming sound, the sound would have to download anew each time it repeats, seriously wasting bandwidth.

A final difference is the way the sounds behave in the Timeline. An event sound works like a movie clip: Once it begins to play, it continues until it's explicitly stopped, even if the SWF file ends in the meantime. A streaming sound works more like a graphic symbol: It plays in synchronization with the Timeline. When the SWF file ends, a streaming sound ends too.

Because they're in frame-by-frame lockstep with the Timeline, streaming sounds are suitable for situations where exact synchronization between animation and sound is important—for example, in scenes with lip-synced dialog, or when the animated action has to match the precise beat of a music track.

Table 7.1 sums up the criteria for deciding whether a sound file should be treated as an event sound or a streaming sound:

Event Sound	Streaming Sound
Short sound file	Long sound file
Suitable for looping	Unsuitable for looping
Independent of Timeline	Synchronized with Timeline

Some of these criteria may contradict each other. For example, if a sound file is long but intended to loop, should it be an event sound or a streaming sound? How about if it needs to loop, but also to be in sync with the Timeline?

There's no right answer in situations like these. Test the movie both ways and see which way it performs better. You can easily switch a sound from event to streaming and back again with no impact on the rest of the movie.

#**60** Putting Sounds in the Timeline

Once you've imported a sound file to the Library, follow these steps to put it in your movie:

1. Create a new layer for the sound in the Timeline. Although this isn't strictly necessary—technically, a sound can share a layer with animation—putting each sound on its own layer is preferable.

2. Insert a keyframe where you want the sound to begin.

3. With the new keyframe selected, either:

   • Choose the name of the sound file from the Sound menu in the Property inspector (**Figure 60a**).

   or

   • Drag an instance of the sound file from the Library onto the Stage. The sound can't be seen on the Stage, but it does appear in the Timeline.

Figure 60a The Sound menu lists all the sound files that are in the Library. Choose one to place that sound in the selected keyframe.

In either case, the sound's waveform appears in the layer, beginning in the designated keyframe (**Figure 60b**).

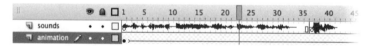

Figure 60b This Timeline shows sounds beginning at frames 1 and 37. (It's fine to have two sounds on the same layer, as long as they're sequential.)

Note
When you attach a sound to a blank keyframe, the circle in the keyframe remains white. A black circle indicates the presence of objects on the Stage, not the presence of sound.

4. With the keyframe still selected, choose either Event (to make the sound an event sound) or Stream (to make it a streaming sound) from the Sync menu in the Property inspector.

The other two options on the Sync menu, Stop and Start, are explained in step 7 and in #61, respectively.

5. To add an effect to the sound, such as a fade or a pan from one channel to the other, choose the effect you want from the Effect menu just above the Sync menu.

6. *For event sounds only:* If you want the sound to repeat a fixed number of times, choose Repeat from the menu to the right of the Sync menu, then enter the desired number of repeats in the next field to the right. (The default setting, Repeat 1 just plays the sound once.)

If you want the sound to loop endlessly, choose Loop instead of Repeat.

7. If you want the sound to end at a particular frame, select that frame in the Timeline and choose Insert > Timeline > Blank Keyframe (or press F7).

That's sufficient to end a streaming sound, but an event sound requires an extra step: With the new blank keyframe still selected, choose Stop from the Sync menu in the Property inspector. Doing so explicitly stops the sound, which—since it's independent of the Timeline—would otherwise continue to play regardless of how many frames are assigned to it.

#61 Managing Looping Sounds

As you'll remember from #35, the default behavior of a SWF file is to loop. If you have a looping sound within a looping SWF file, the result can be chaotic.

Consider, for example, the Timeline shown in **Figure 61a**. Assume that the waveform represents a 15-frame-long event sound that's set to loop. Here's what happens when you play the movie's SWF file:

Figure 61a The sound that begins in frame 6 is a looping event sound that's 15 frames long.

1. At frame 1, the animation begins.

2. At frame 6, the sound begins. Because it's an event sound and therefore independent of the Timeline, it will loop continuously unless something stops it.

3. At frame 21, the sound repeats.

4. At frame 22, the animation ends. The movie loops back and plays again from frame 1.

5. At frame 6, the sound begins. However, the sound that began at frame 21 during the first run of the movie is still playing. There are now *two* instances of the sound playing at the same time.

From here on, every time the movie repeats, a new instance of the sound is added to the others that are already looping, with their start times staggered by seven frames. The result is an endless (and unbearable) stack of sound upon sound.

The way to avoid this problem is to use a special type of event sound called a *start* sound. Before it begins to play, a start sound checks whether any other instances of the same sound are already playing. If so, it stays silent.

To convert a sound to a start sound, select the keyframe in which the sound begins and choose Start from the Sync menu in the Property inspector.

For this example, let's imagine that the sound beginning in frame 6 is now a start sound. When we play the movie, steps 1 through 4 are the same as before. However, in step 5, the start sound detects that another instance is already playing, and so it doesn't play. The result is a single looping sound rather than cacophony.

#**62** Synchronizing Sound to Animation

By default, Flash Player plays every frame of a SWF file, no matter how long it takes. Because some frames take longer to download, or make extra demands on the computer's processor, Flash movies often don't play at a steady rate.

The speed variations in a movie's playback are usually too subtle to notice. The addition of sound, however, adds an extra challenge. Sound—and music in particular—demands a fixed, steady playback speed. Speed-ups, slowdowns, and gaps are unacceptable. For this reason, one of Flash Player's top priorities is to make sure that sound plays back smoothly and without interruption, regardless of what's happening on the Stage.

This policy has different consequences for event sounds than for streaming sounds. While an event sound plays back at a steady rate, the visual portion of the movie continues to speed up and slow down according to the demands of each frame. As a result, an event sound and the rest of the Timeline line up only at one point: the keyframe in which the sound begins to play. After that, the sound and the action may drift apart fairly quickly.

For this reason, event sounds are best used in situations where extended synchronization isn't needed. In the case of a car collision, for example, it's important that the crash sound starts at the same moment as the impact shown on the Stage, but after that, it doesn't matter how precisely the sounds of buckling metal and shattering glass match the animation.

When playing back streaming sounds, however, Flash Player uses a different strategy. A streaming sound is locked to the Timeline frame by frame, so that, for example, a character's speech and mouth movements are synchronized; it wouldn't be acceptable for the character's mouth to be ending one sentence while the voice has gone on to the next. Since sound playback takes priority, Flash skips animation frames wherever necessary to keep the sound and the action in sync. The price for precise synchronization is occasional jumps in the animation.

Because of these differences, syncing with event sounds and with streaming sounds demands different strategies on your part. When you're working with event sounds, the best approach is to do the animation first and add the sound later. You can scrub through the movie and see exactly where a rock hits the water, then insert a keyframe at that point to trigger the sound of the splash.

(continued on next page)

When you're working with streaming sounds, it's often preferable to create the soundtrack first and then create animation to match it. For example, if you want a character's dance movements to match the rhythm of a piece of music, put the music in the Timeline first. By looking at the waveform, you can see where each beat of the music falls (**Figure 62a**). You can then pace the animation so that the keyframes for each movement coincide with the musical beats.

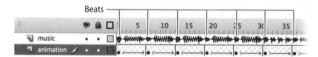

Figure 62a Once you find the steady rhythm in the waveform for a piece of music, you can insert keyframes in another layer to match the animation to the beat.

#63 Setting Sound Properties

As with bitmaps (see #55), Flash allows you to set properties individually for each sound file you import. There's no need to do this for every sound file, however; Flash pays attention to a sound file's properties only if it's used as an event sound. For streaming sounds, Flash uses the global sound settings in Publish Settings (see #77).

To open the Sound Properties dialog box, select a sound file in the Library and either double-click its icon or click the Properties icon at the bottom of the Library panel (**Figure 63a**).

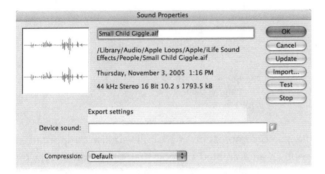

Figure 63a Most of the elements in the Sound Properties dialog box are similar to those in the Bitmap Properties dialog box.

The first option in the dialog box, "Device sound," applies only to mobile devices using the Flash Lite player (a stripped-down version of the standard Flash Player). If you're creating Flash movies to be viewed on traditional computers, you can ignore this field.

The second option, Compression, is more important. This menu determines how Flash will compress the sound for inclusion in the movie's SWF file. The menu choices are:

- **Default.** This choice tells Flash to apply the global compression settings in Publish Settings. (If the sound file is used only as a streaming sound, Flash will do that anyway.) Since event sounds should be as small as possible for quick download, you'll usually want to apply more than the default amount of compression to them.

- **ADPCM.** This is an old-style form of compression that's included mainly for compatibility with early versions of Flash Player. It's sometimes

(continued on next page)

effective for very short sounds, but in most other cases, MP3 compression yields better results.

- **MP3.** Whether you're compressing sound effects, music, or speech, MP3 will almost always give you the highest quality with the lowest file size. If you choose MP3 compression for a file that's already in MP3 format, a check box labeled "Use imported MP3 quality" appears above the menu (**Figure 63b**). Deselecting the check box allows Flash to recompress the file, which may result in reduced sound quality.

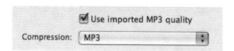

Figure 63b This check box appears only if MP3 is selected in the Compression menu, and only for a sound file that's already in MP3 format.

- **Raw.** This means no compression at all. If file size isn't important in your movie—if it's an animated cartoon that will go on a DVD, for example—uncompressed sound will give you the best quality. But if you're creating movies for the Web, Raw is not practical.

- **Speech.** Like ADPCM, this is an old form of compression that's usually inferior to MP3. Use it only for movies that need to be compatible with Flash Player version 3 or earlier.

Choosing any of these menu items causes additional settings to display at the bottom of the dialog box. Since MP3 is the most common choice, we'll look at those settings, but the explanations here can be applied to other forms of compression as well.

Note
For files that were already in MP3 format when you imported them, the following options appear only if you deselect the "Use imported MP3 quality" check box.

- **Preprocessing.** The "Convert stereo to mono" check box is selected by default, but it can be deselected for bit rates of 20 kbps (kilobits per second) or more. Use stereo sound only when necessary; as mentioned in #58, it can double the size of the SWF file.

- **Bit rate.** This setting is different from the bit-rate setting in most sound-editing programs, which determines how much information is used to describe each sound sample. In Flash, *bit rate* refers to how many kilobits (1,000 bits) of sound information that Flash Player has to process each second. Higher bit rates yield higher sound quality, but they also yield larger SWF files and possibly reduced performance. The default of 16 kbps is usually the lowest bit rate that's acceptable for music.

- **Quality.** A setting of Fast reduces processing time at the expense of sound quality; Best does the opposite; and Medium compromises between the two. In most cases, the Quality setting doesn't matter very much; the difference in processing time generally isn't noticeable, and neither is the difference in quality.

At any time, you can click the Test button to play your sound with the current compression settings. The text at the bottom of the dialog box will tell you the predicted file size and the degree of compression. As with bitmaps, you have to use trial and error to find the best trade-off between file size and quality.

#64 Editing Sounds

It's highly recommended that you edit your sound files in a real sound-editing program before you import them to Flash. However, Flash does offer some elementary tools for modifying sounds. To get to them, select a keyframe that contains a sound in the Timeline, then click the Edit button in the Property inspector, located to the right of the Effects button.

Note
There's no way to edit a sound file globally in Flash; you can edit only instances of sounds in the Timeline. Editing one instance has no effect on the others.

An Edit Envelope dialog box appears, revealing the sound-editing controls (**Figure 64a**). The dialog box is accurately labeled Edit Envelope rather than Edit Sound because you can't change the content of the sound file; all you can do is change the size and shape of the metaphorical container that holds it.

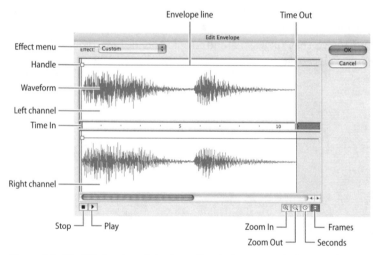

Figure 64a The Edit Envelope dialog box offers the basic controls that you'd find in any sound-editing program.

The dialog box displays the sound's waveform in two panes: The upper pane represents the computer's left sound channel; the lower pane represents the right channel. If the sound is stereo, the waveforms in the two panes are different; if it's mono, they're the same.

A time scale runs between the two panes. By clicking either of the two icons at the lower-right corner of the dialog box, you can control whether the scale displays seconds or frames. To trim unwanted material at the beginning or end of the sound, slide the Time In and Time Out markers along the scale.

Tip

The portions of the sound that you cut out with the Time In and Time Out markers will be excluded from the SWF file. Trimming your sounds down to what's absolutely necessary is one of the best ways to reduce a movie's file size.

The horizontal black line above each waveform is called the *envelope line*; it controls the volume of the sound. You can reduce the overall volume by using the handles to drag each envelope line downward. To adjust the volume differently for different parts of the waveform, click anywhere along either of the envelope lines to create new handles (**Figure 64b**). Adding a handle to one line automatically adds a corresponding handle to the other.

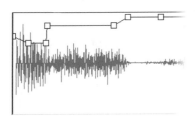

Figure 64b You can smooth out a sound by reducing the volume of the louder portions and boosting the volume of the softer portions.

Some commonly used envelope patterns, such as fading in and fading out, can be chosen from the Effects menu. (It's identical to the Effects menu in the Property inspector.) Choosing an effect causes the handles and envelope lines to jump to the appropriate positions—but any manual editing that you've done will be wiped out in the process. Going in the other direction is fine; you can use an effect as a starting point and then tweak it manually.

#65 Adding Sounds to Buttons

As we discussed in #27, users expect some sort of feedback when they click a button. The feedback can be visual (a change in color, for example), but the addition of a confirming click or a beep is especially satisfying to most users.

To attach a sound to a button:

1. Import an appropriate sound file to the Library. The most effective button sounds are less than half a second in length and have no empty space at the beginning of the sound file.

2. Double-click a button symbol in the Library or on the Stage to place it in editing mode. You'll see the familiar four-frame timeline (**Figure 65a**).

3. Click the Insert Layer icon to add a new layer to the timeline.

4. Select the Down cell of the new layer and press F6 or F7 to insert a keyframe.

Figure 65a To make a button beep or click, attach an event sound to a keyframe in the Down cell.

5. Drag an instance of the button sound to the Stage, or select its name from the Sound menu in the Property inspector.

6. Choose Event from the Sync menu. (A button sound should always be an event sound.)

7. Click Scene 1 in the breadcrumb trail to exit symbol-editing mode.

8. Choose Control > Enable Simple Buttons and test the button.

Although it's technically possible to attach a sound to the Over state as well, it's best to avoid doing so (except perhaps as part of a game). Users generally find it annoying to have a button make noise when they roll over it.

Don't Try This at Home

It's not clear why anyone would want to do these things, but:

- Attaching a sound to a button's Up keyframe causes the sound to play when the user rolls the pointer out of the button.

- Attaching a sound to a button's Hit keyframe causes the sound to play when the user releases (not depresses) the mouse button.

CHAPTER EIGHT

Working with Video

Video has become one of the most popular features in Flash. This is partly because of the growth in high-speed access to the Internet—more than 70 percent of active U.S. Internet users now have broadband connections—but it's also because Flash video is so easy to use. Flash video works identically on any computer that has a recent version of Flash Player. And because Flash video can be controlled by ActionScript, any developer can easily create a custom video player that fits the look and style of a particular Flash movie. It's no wonder that popular video sites such as YouTube and MySpaceTV use Flash Video (aka FLV) as their delivery format. This chapter gives you the basics of getting video into your Flash movie and making it playable on the Web.

#66 Getting Familiar with Digital Video

To work effectively with video in Flash, it's helpful to know a few things about digital video in general.

Fundamentally, all digital video is a succession of bitmapped images, each visible for a fraction of a second (**Figure 66a**). As with animation, the slight changes from one frame of video to the next give the illusion of motion. The differences between video file formats have to do with how the bitmaps are compressed and stored.

Figure 66a Each frame of digital video is a bitmapped image. Because displaying so many bitmaps so quickly requires a powerful processor and a fast hard drive, it's only recently that most home computers have become capable of playing full-screen, full-motion video.

The most familiar video formats on the Web are QuickTime (MOV), Windows Media (WMV), and Real Media (RM). Each requires its own player, and although all are cross-platform, QuickTime has closer ties to the Mac, and Windows Media to the PC. Many Web sites make their video content available in multiple formats, because there's no way to predict which player (or players) a user might have.

Having the right player isn't necessarily enough. Nearly every video file online uses some sort of compression to keep the file size manageable. There are many different compression schemes, each of which is embodied in a file called a *compressor/decompressor*—a *codec* for short. Some codecs are built into the standard video players, but others have to be installed separately. If a video file is created using a certain codec, it can be viewed only with that codec.

To get around these obstacles, Flash introduced its own proprietary video format, Flash Video (FLV). Video files in any other format have to be converted to FLV for Flash to use them (see #67). Unlike QuickTime, which offers a choice of about 20 codecs, FLV uses only two codecs: Sorenson Spark (which requires Flash Player 7 or later) and On2 VP6 (which requires Flash Player 8 or later).

This uniformity allows FLV to come close to being a universal Web video format. Flash Player is installed on nearly all Macs and PCs, and Adobe supports a version for Linux as well. Because the player software is the same, Flash video looks and acts the same way on each platform.

Note
Unlike MOV, WMV, and RM files, each of which can be viewed in its respective player, FLV files can't be opened directly in Flash Player. An FLV file has to be either embedded in or linked to a SWF file.

Compression Digression

To make video files small and more easily playable, most codecs use both *image compression* and *temporal compression*. You're already familiar with image compression; we applied it to imported photos in #55. When you consider what a difference it made to apply JPEG compression to a single bitmap, imagine how much disk space you can save by applying similar compression to each of the thousands of bitmaps in a typical video file.

Image compression works by throwing away nonessential information without changing the overall appearance of a bitmap. Temporal compression uses a different principle: Although each frame in a video file is slightly different from the others, some elements remain the same. For example, in a talking-head interview, the subject's lip movements and facial expressions change from frame to frame, but the background stays still. By limiting the information stored in each frame to what has changed since the previous frame, temporal compression eliminates a tremendous amount of redundancy.

#67 Importing Video Files

As with audio files, it's best to edit your video files before importing them into Flash. As you'll see in #69, Flash does have some rudimentary video-editing features, but you can accomplish much more in a program such as Apple iMovie or Microsoft Windows Movie Maker (**Figure 67a**).

Figure 67a Your computer already has video-editing software: iMovie (shown here) on the Mac, or Windows Movie Maker on the PC.

Save your edited video with the least compression allowed by your software and disk space—if possible, with no compression at all. Flash does its own compression when you import the video file, and recompressing already compressed video degrades image quality.

Flash can't import video on its own; it needs help from other software. On a Mac, you must have QuickTime 7 or later; in Windows, you must have DirectX 9 or later. Because of this dependence, Flash imports different video formats on each platform. On a Mac, it accepts files in AVI, DV, MPEG, and MOV format; on a PC, it accepts files in AVI, MPEG, WMV, and ASF format. If you have QuickTime installed on your PC, Flash will import the Mac file formats as well.

You're already familiar with the import dialog boxes that Flash uses with certain types of vector and bitmap files. Because video is so much more complex, Flash gives you not just a dialog box, but a whole *series* of dialog boxes—collectively known as the Video Import wizard—that guide you through importing a video file.

Direct *What?*

DirectX is a collection of dynamic linking libraries, or DLLs, that Windows applications use to interact with the computer. When you bought your computer, the vendor installed a suitable set of DLLs that handle the translation between the software and hardware.

DirectX isn't updated automatically through Windows Update, so you may not know whether you have a recent enough version for Flash to use for video import. To find out in Windows Vista, type run in the Start Search box in the Start menu; then choose Run from the resulting list. (In Windows XP or earlier, choose Run directly from the Start menu.) Type dxdiag in the Run command box and press Enter to open the DirectX Diagnostic Tool window. Click the System tab and look for DirectX version 9 or later near the bottom of the list. If you need to update, you can do so on Microsoft's Web site.

To begin the process, choose File > Import > Import Video. You could also choose Import to Stage or Import to Library; if you select a video file to import, Flash recognizes it and launches the Video Import wizard.

The first screen of the Video Import wizard asks you to locate the file you want to import. Select a file on your computer or a file that you've uploaded to your Web server, then click Next (Windows) or Continue (Mac).

That's the easy part. Since the rest of the Video Import wizard requires more detailed information, the remaining screens will be covered as separate topics.

#68 Choosing a Deployment Method

The second screen of the Video Import wizard asks you how you want to deploy your video. *Deploy* is an odd word in this context; what the wizard really wants to know is where you plan to put the video file. The options are:

- **Progressive download from a Web server.** This is the most common choice. Your video remains in a separate file; Flash converts it to FLV format and links it to the SWF file. You upload both files to your Web server. When a user plays your SWF file, Flash Player treats it like a streaming sound: It downloads just enough of the video file to begin playing it and continues to download the file behind the scenes (**Figure 68a**).

Progress bar

Figure 68a In the "skinned" version of the video player (see #71), a progress bar indicates how much of a video file has been downloaded.

- **Stream from Flash Video Streaming Service; Stream from Flash Media Server.** The word *streaming* can be used loosely to describe files that begin to play while still downloading—we've used it that way in this book. Strictly speaking, however, streaming requires two-way communication between the server and the client computer. For true streaming of Flash video, you need Flash Media Server, which monitors the speed of the Internet connection and adjusts the stream's data rate accordingly; it also responds to commands such as fast forward, rewind, and seek. Large organizations often have their own Flash Media Server, in which case "Stream from Flash Media Server" is the appropriate choice; individuals and organizations who have accounts with a hosted streaming service should choose "Stream from Flash Video Streaming Service."

- **As mobile device video bundled in SWF.** This option is for video that's intended to be played on a mobile device (such as a cell phone) using the Flash Lite player.

- **Embed video in SWF and play in timeline.** In older versions of Flash, video was stored in the Library, dragged to the Timeline, and played from inside the SWF file, just like bitmaps and sounds. Now that streaming and progressive download are available, this option is not used much, but it's still a convenient way to handle short video clips.

- **Linked QuickTime video for publishing to QuickTime.** Not all Flash movies are intended for the Web. Some are animation or special-effects sequences that will be included in a film or video; some are self-contained animated cartoons made for broadcast or distribution on DVD. In those cases, the finished movie is exported to a QuickTime file rather than SWF, and linked video files can be in QuickTime format rather than FLV.

When you've made your choice, click Next (Windows) or Continue (Mac).

If you've chosen "Embed video in SWF and play in timeline," the Video Import wizard takes you to the Embedding dialog box, which is covered in #69. If you've chosen another option, you can skip to #70, which deals with the Encoding dialog box.

#69 Choosing Embedding Options

Adobe discourages the embedding of video in Flash movies, and for good reasons: Embedded video bloats the SWF file, has to be downloaded in its entirety before it can be played, and frequently has audio synchronization problems. It also demands a lot of memory, and if the user's computer doesn't have it, Flash Player may crash. To minimize these problems, Adobe recommends that embedded video be limited to clips less than 10 seconds long.

However, there are also some good reasons to embed video. Embedded video is easy to work with: Each frame of video corresponds to a frame in the Timeline (**Figure 69a**), allowing you to synchronize events in your movie to the action in the video without using ActionScript (see #70). You don't have to remember to upload multiple files to your Web server, because everything is contained in a single SWF file. Best of all, Flash offers editing features for embedded video that aren't available for the other deployment methods.

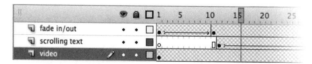

Figure 69a When you put your video in the Timeline, you can synchronize animation to it just as you would with a streaming sound (see #62). Unlike streaming sounds, however, embedded video doesn't stream; it has to be fully downloaded before it can play.

The Embedding screen in the Video Import wizard offers these options:

- **Symbol type.** If you choose Embedded Video, your imported video is stored in the Library as a video file. You can, however, choose to import the video as a movie clip or graphic symbol. Importing it as a movie clip allows the video to play independently of the main Timeline (see #28). There's no real advantage to importing it as a graphic symbol.

- **Audio track.** The default choice is Integrated, which means that the video and its audio track are in a single file. The other option is Separate, which brings in the video and audio as separate items in the Library. Keeping the audio track separate allows you to do cutaways (letting the audio in a scene continue while the video cuts briefly to something else), but it also makes you responsible for keeping the video and audio synchronized.

- **Place instance on stage; Expand timeline if needed.** When these options are selected (as they are by default), Flash puts the imported video both on the Stage and in the Library. It places the video in a keyframe in the Timeline and inserts enough frames to play the video. If you deselect "Place instance on stage," the video file is imported only to the Library.

- **Embed the entire video.** This option is self-explanatory.

- **Edit video first.** If you choose "Edit video first" and click Next (Windows) or Continue (Mac), you're taken to a simple editing screen (**Figure 69b**). You can click the Add icon in the left pane to create differently named clips and give each one its own start and end points, effectively turning one video file into several. Use the In and Out markers to designate the beginning and end of each clip, then click "Update clip" to apply the edits.

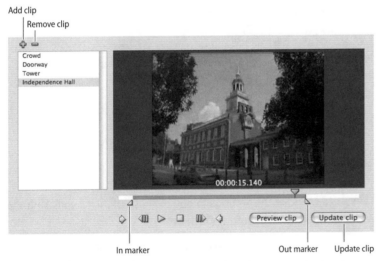

Figure 69b This convenient but little-known "editing studio" is available only for embedded video.

After you've made your choices, click Next (Windows) or Continue (Mac) to go to the encoding screen.

#70 Setting Encoding Options

Before Flash can convert your video file to the Flash Video (FLV) format, it needs input from you: for example, which codec you want to use, how much compression you want to apply, and at what frame rate you want the video to play. Applying these settings as the video is converted to FLV format is known as *encoding* the video. You supply the necessary information on the Encoding screen of the Video Import wizard.

Note
If the file you're importing is already in FLV format, the Video Import wizard will skip this step.

The easiest way to specify encoding options is to use the Profiles menu (**Figure 70a**). Each profile is a bundle of video and audio settings designed to fit a particular audience. For example, if your Web site is aimed at frugal families, many of whom have old computers and dial-up connections, you might choose the Flash 7-Modem Quality profile. If your Web site is directed at corporate executives, you might go for the Flash 8-High Quality profile.

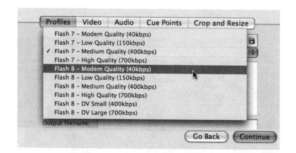

Figure 70a The Profiles menu in the Video Import wizard displays these profiles, each intended for a different audience.

You can modify the settings in any of these profiles by clicking the Video or Audio tab. The settings include:

- **Video.** You can choose between the Sorensen Spark codec or the On2 VP6 codec. If your video was created with a transparent background, as is possible in Adobe After Effects, you have to use the On2 VP6 codec and check "Encode Alpha Channel" to preserve the transparency.

Seven Is Heaven; Eight Is Great

The version numbers in the encoding profiles—Flash 7 and Flash 8—refer to the oldest version of Flash Player that's can play your FLV file. None of the profiles mention Flash 9 because files that can be played in Flash Player 7 or 8 will also play in any later version.

How do you know whether to select 7 or 8? According to Adobe's statistics, more people have Flash Player 7 installed—but only about 2 percent more. The bigger difference is technical: If you're targeting version 7, you have to use an older codec, Sorensen Spark; if you're targeting version 8, you can use a newer codec, On2 VP6. Sorensen Spark delivers slightly lower video quality but encodes and decodes more quickly; On2 VP6 offers higher quality but takes longer to encode and decode, which might affect your video's performance on older computers.

- **Frame rate.** For best quality, the encoded video should have the same frame rate as the original video file. (This is the default choice, and is the *only* choice if you chose "Embed video in SWF" as your deployment option.) To make your video less processor-intensive, you can choose a lower frame rate.

- **Quality** and **Max[imum] data rate.** If your intended audience has fast computers and broadband Internet connections, you can choose High; if they are more likely to have dial-up connections, you should choose Low. Medium is a good compromise for general audiences (**Figure 70b**). Each quality setting puts a different data rate into the "Max data rate" field. If you wish, you can enter your own data rate; doing so changes the Quality setting to Custom.

Figure 70b A frame of video is shown at low quality (left), medium quality (center), and high quality (right).

- **Keyframe placement** and **Keyframe interval.** *Keyframe* has a different meaning in digital video than it does in animation: It refers to a complete frame of video that's used as a reference point for temporal compression. (See "Compression Digression" in #66.) The more keyframes you have in your video, the better it will look—but having fewer keyframes reduces the file size. The default is Automatic, which gives Flash permission to decide how many keyframes there should be and where to put them. This is almost always the best option, but you can specify a fixed interval by choosing Custom for "Keyframe placement" and entering a number of frames in "Keyframe interval."

- **Audio.** You can't choose an audio codec; MP3 compression is the only option. You can, however, set a bit rate (see #63).

(continued on next page)

Tip
Although the video encoder that's built into Flash is easy to use, its features are limited. If you want more options—such as a choice of audio codecs—you can use a third-party program such as Sorensen Squeeze to do your encoding.

The last two tabs in the Encoding dialog box allow you to set cue points and to crop or resize the video. *Cue points* are invisible markers that you can insert anywhere in the video. You can use ActionScript to assign events to these cue points, so that things can happen on the Stage in sync with the action of the video. Cropping and resizing are self-explanatory, but as previously mentioned, it's better to do these things in your video-editing program.

When you're finished with the Encoding dialog box, click Next (Windows) or Continue (Mac).

If you've chosen "Embed video in SWF and play in timeline" as your deployment method, you're at the end of the process. When you click Finish, your video file is imported to the Library, and placed on the Stage and in the Timeline if appropriate.

If you're using one of the other deployment methods, your next stop is the Skinning screen.

#71 Choosing a Skin for the Video Player

The FLVPlayback component—known informally as the *video player*—is what displays your video on the Stage. Normally, to use the interface components that come with Flash, you have to write ActionScript (see Chapter 11). In this case, however, no scripting is required; all you have to do is choose a skin for the player.

Skin is a somewhat misleading term. Applying a skin to an object usually means changing its outward appearance only; its functionality remains the same. In this case, however, your choice of skin determines what the player is able to do.

The Video Import wizard's Skinning screen lets you choose from 34 different skins. They vary by size, type of video controls, and where they're positioned in relation to the video (**Figure 71a**). Each skin is itself a Flash movie.

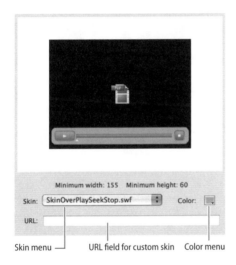

Figure 71a Each skin is named for what it does. For example, SkinOverPlaySeekStop.swf indicates that the control bar is superimposed over the video rather than placed beneath it, and that the player has Play, Seek, and Stop controls.

To the right of the Skin menu is a standard Flash color menu from which you can choose a skin color. A preview window lets you see the skin and use its controls, but your video doesn't appear there, and the controls don't have any effect.

Some advanced Flash users design their own skins instead of using the ones supplied by Flash. (Designing a custom skin is not a trivial task; it's not something you should try until you're very familiar with Flash and ActionScript.) To use a custom skin, enter the URL of its SWF file in the field below the menus.

(continued on next page)

If you don't want your movie's audience to interact with the video, you can choose None from the Skin menu, allowing the video to appear on the Stage as a plain rectangle with no controls.

When you've selected a skin, click Next (Windows) or Continue (Mac). You're taken to a screen that summarizes your encoding decisions. Click Finish, and Flash encodes your video, bringing the import process to an end. In the folder where your FLA file resides, you'll now find an FLV file containing your video. If you've chosen a skin for the video player, the skin's SWF file is added to the folder when you test or publish the movie. You'll have to upload both of these new files to your Web server.

#72 Using a Video Clip in Your Movie

After you've imported and encoded a video file, you'll find a new item in the Library: the video file itself, if you've embedded the video; or the FLVPlayback component, if you've chosen another deployment method. Both of these items work like other "symboloids": You can drag multiple instances to the Stage or embed them in symbols; you can use the Free Transform tool to scale, rotate, or skew those instances (**Figure 72a**); you can even motion-tween instances. (Actually, motion-tweening the FLVPlayback component doesn't work, but if you embed the video player in a movie clip, you can motion-tween an instance of the movie clip.)

Figure 72a A video instance can play normally even if it's been scaled, rotated, or skewed.

However, the rule that you learned in childhood applies: Just because you *can* do something doesn't mean you *should* do it.

Watching video—not to mention starting and stopping it—is difficult when the video is rotated, skewed, or moving around the Stage. More important are the technical limitations: Playing back video in a Flash movie puts a big load on the computer's processor; playing back video that's been transformed or animated can challenge even a powerful computer. It's best just to put the video somewhere on the Stage and leave it there.

If you must animate or transform a video instance, you can reduce its demand on the user's computer by keeping the video's frame rate low and its dimensions small. Scaling down the video on the Stage doesn't help; you have to *import* it already scaled down, using the crop/resize feature on the Encoding tab of the Video Import wizard (see #70).

If you haven't embedded your video, you can change some characteristics of the video player by using a panel called the Component Inspector. For example, the default behavior of the FLVPlayback component is to start playing the video as soon as an instance of the player appears on

(continued on next page)

the Stage. In some cases, however, you may want the video to remain paused until the user clicks Play. To make that change, select the video player on the Stage and choose Window > Component Inspector. On the Parameters tab of the Component Inspector (**Figure 72b**), change the value of the "autoPlay" parameter from true to false. But do this only if your video player has a skin with a Play button; otherwise, there's no way for the user to start the video.

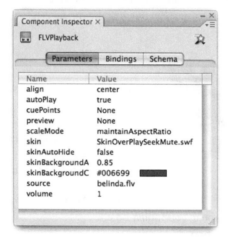

Figure 72b The Component Inspector displays parameters and values for a selected instance of any component—in this case, the FLVPlayback component.

Some of the parameters in the Component Inspector call for technical expertise, but others are easy to change. For example, use the skin parameter to change the player's skin; use the skinBackground Color or skinBackgroundAlpha parameter to change the color or opacity of the skin; and use the volume parameter to set the initial volume of the video's audio track. (To do this, enter a number between 0 and 1, where 0 represents silence and 1 represents full volume.) If you move the FLV file that's linked to the player, use the source parameter to tell Flash where to find it.

#73 Updating Video Files

Once you've encoded your video file as Flash Video, you can't make any more changes in it. No video-editing program works directly on FLV files—not even Adobe Premiere Pro. If you want to change anything in the video, you have to open the original video file in the editing program of your choice, resave it in its original format, and re-encode it for Flash.

If your movie uses a linked FLV file, you can accomplish this without having to redo anything in your movie:

1. Use the Video Import wizard or an external program, such as Quick-Time Pro or the Flash Video Encoder, to convert the revised video file to FLV format.

2. In your movie, select the video player on the Stage and use the source parameter in the Component Inspector to replace the original file with the new one.

    or

    Outside of Flash, go to the folder where the old FLV file resides and replace it with the new FLV file, making sure to keep the same file-name. Flash will use the new file without knowing that anything has changed.

If your movie uses embedded video, the process is slightly different:

1. When you edit the video file, save the revised version to the same folder as the original, and give it the same filename. In other words, overwrite the original. (You'll probably want to make a backup copy of the original first.)

(continued on next page)

2. In the Library, double-click your embedded video file to open the Video Properties dialog box (**Figure 73a**).

3. Click the Update button in the dialog box. Flash replaces the embedded video with the new version.

Note
Don't use the Import button. It imports only FLV files.

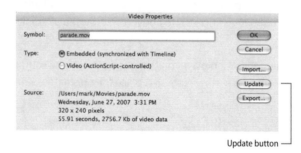

Update button

Figure 73a The Update button in the Video Properties dialog box replaces embedded video with a new version, so long as the new version has the same filename as the old one.

#74 Using the Flash Video Encoder

The Flash Video Encoder is a separate application that's installed on your hard drive when you install Flash. Like the Video Import wizard, the Flash Video Encoder converts files in a variety of formats to FLV. Unlike the Video Import wizard, it can convert multiple files at once, in a process called *batch encoding*.

To use it:

1. Locate the Flash Video Encoder application—it's in the same folder as Flash. Double-click its icon to launch the program. (In Windows, you can also launch it from the Start menu.)

   The Flash Video Encoder window appears (**Figure 74a**).

List of files to be encoded   Successfully encoded

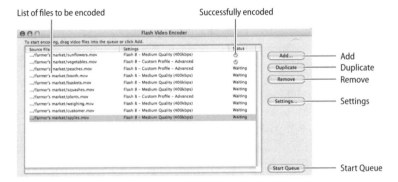

Figure 74a This is the upper portion of the Flash Video Encoder window.

2. Drag one or more video files into the window's list area, or click the Add button to navigate to the files that you want to convert.

3. From the list, select one or more files to which you want to apply the same encoding settings. To select multiple files, click the first one and Control-click (Windows) or Command-click (Mac) the additional ones.

4. Click Settings. A Flash Video Encoding Settings dialog box appears, allowing you to choose a profile and/or modify individual settings. (The dialog box is identical to the Encoding screen in the Video Import wizard—see #70.)

5. Click OK to apply the settings to the selected files.

(continued on next page)

6. Repeat steps 3 through 5 to assign settings to any remaining files. Files to which you don't assign settings will use the defaults.

7. Click Start Queue. The Flash Video Encoder converts the files one by one, giving you progress reports in the lower portion of the window. As each file is converted, the new FLV file is placed in the same folder as the original.

When the batch is complete, all the files in the list will have green check marks next to them.

8. Files on the list don't disappear, even when you quit the Flash Video Encoder and open it again. To remove files manually, select them and click Remove.

CHAPTER NINE

Publishing and Exporting

Converting a Flash movie into a format suitable for public consumption is called *publishing*. Effective publishing requires that you know as much as possible about your movie's likely viewers: What kind of computers are they likely to have? How fast are their Internet connections? What version of Flash Player can you expect them to have? The answers to questions like these help you choose the most appropriate output options for a movie. Those options—called *Publish Settings*—are stored in the movie's FLA file.

Flash also has the capacity to convert movies—or single frames—into a variety of file formats through a process called *exporting*. The advantage of exporting over publishing is that more file formats are available; the disadvantage is that export settings are not saved in the FLA file.

The emphasis of this chapter will be on publishing for the Web, although we'll also look briefly at other distribution media.

#75 Choosing a Publishing Format

The first step in publishing a movie is deciding how you plan to distribute it. Will the movie be posted on the Web, burned to a DVD, e-mailed, displayed continuously on a public kiosk, or presented to your audience in some other way? Each distribution method requires a suitable file format.

To select a distribution format for your movie, choose File > Publish Settings. In the Publish Settings dialog box, click the Formats tab (if it's not selected already) and select one or more of the following formats:

- **Flash (.swf); HTML (.html).** Both of these options are selected by default, because most Flash movies are published for the Web. See #76 for an explanation of how SWF and HTML files work together on a Web site.

- **GIF image (.gif).** Before Flash, most animation on the Web was in GIF format. Unlike SWF files, GIF files don't require a plug-in; any Web browser can play an animated GIF. The drawbacks are that the GIF format doesn't work very well with photos or gradients (**Figure 75a**); it doesn't support sound; and its file sizes are often impractically large because each frame is a separate bitmap. Nevertheless, GIF is still used occasionally for short, simple animations. Flash allows an entire movie to be saved as an animated GIF or a single frame to be saved as a static GIF.

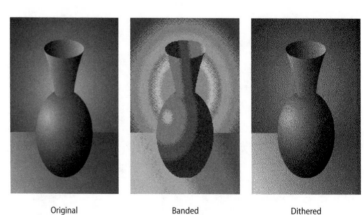

Original   Banded   Dithered

Figure 75a A GIF file supports only 256 colors. If an object contains more colors than that, it will appear banded when converted to GIF format. You can avoid banding by choosing one of the Dither options, which allow Flash to simulate missing colors by interspersing dots of available colors.

- **JPEG image (.jpg); PNG image (.png).** For information on these single-image bitmapped formats, see #83.

- **Windows projector (.exe); Macintosh projector.** These are Flash movies in the form of stand-alone, executable files. For more information, see #81.

- **QuickTime with Flash track (.mov).** This special type of QuickTime file is covered in #82.

Each format has options that you can set by clicking the appropriate tab at the top of the Publish Settings dialog box (**Figure 75b**). We'll cover options for SWF and HTML files; you can learn about the others from the Flash Help system.

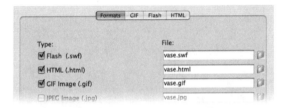

Figure 75b The leftmost tab in Publish Settings is always Formats. The remaining tabs vary according to which file formats you've selected.

By default, published files are saved in the same folder as the FLA file they're generated from. To specify a different name or location for a file, use the File field to the right of each format in Publish Settings.

#76 Linking SWF Files to HTML Files

Standard Web pages are coded in HTML, which can be created in a text-editing program, because HTML consists of plain text. Elements such as graphics, video, and Flash movies aren't part of the HTML file; they're uploaded separately to the Web server. The HTML code includes pointers to those external files that tell the browser where and how to display them on the page.

When you publish a SWF file, Flash creates an HTML file containing the code needed to display the Flash movie in a browser. The exact content of this file depends on the HTML options you choose in Publish Settings (see #78). Even at the default settings, the code isn't trivial: Although a still image can be placed on a page with a single HTML tag, a SWF movie requires a paragraph's worth of HTML to play reliably (**Figure 76a**).

Code to display a SWF file

```
<noscript>
    <object classid="clsid:d27cdb6e-ae6d-11cf-96b8-444553540000" codebase=
"http://download.macromedia.com/pub/shockwave/cabs/flash/swflash.cab#version=9,0,0,0"
 width="550" height="400" id="myMovie" align="middle">
    <param name="allowScriptAccess" value="sameDomain" />
    <param name="allowFullScreen" value="false" />
    <param name="movie" value="myMovie.swf" /><param name="quality" value="high" />
<param name="bgcolor" value="#ffffff" />    <embed src="myMovie.swf" quality="high"
bgcolor="#ffffff" width="550" height="400" name="myMovie" align="middle"
allowScriptAccess="sameDomain" allowFullScreen="false" type=
"application/x-shockwave-flash" pluginspage=
"http://www.macromedia.com/go/getflashplayer" />
    </object>
</noscript>
<img src="myImage.gif" width="550" height="400">
</body>
</html>
```

Code to display a GIF image

Figure 76a This HTML file illustrates the complexity of the code needed to display a Flash movie as compared to a still image.

Cut Out the Middleman?

When you include a Flash movie in a Web page, you need an HTML file for the page and a SWF file for the movie. But what if your movie *is* the Web page? Why not skip the HTML file, use an address such as www.myDomain.com/myFlashMovie.swf, and let the SWF file open directly in the user's browser?

Here's what happens when you don't use an HTML file:

- You have no control over how the movie is displayed in the browser: what its dimensions are, how it scales, and where it appears in the browser window.
- You lose the opportunity to do Flash detection (see #80).
- Your page won't be indexed or listed by search engines.

The Web page created by the Flash HTML file is a bare-bones affair: All it does is show your movie against a solid-color background. If you want other content to appear on the Web page, you have three options:

- Add more HTML code to the file that Flash created, either by hand or by using the Web-page editing program of your choice.

- Copy the necessary code from the Flash HTML file and paste it into another Web page that has the content you want. (This option requires some familiarity with HTML.)

- If you have Dreamweaver, use it to create your Web page. When you import the SWF file, Dreamweaver automatically inserts the HTML code to play it, making the Flash HTML file unnecessary.

Suspenders vs. Satay

The expression "belt and suspenders" is used to describe someone who's so cautious that he wears both a belt *and* suspenders to hold his pants up. When it comes to displaying SWF files, Flash uses a belt, suspenders, and a few safety pins as well. Its HTML code repeats the same instructions several times in different ways to ensure that a SWF file will play in every browser under any possible circumstances. While Adobe intends this code to be thorough, an increasing number of people have complained that it's written inefficiently and includes tags and syntax that are no longer considered valid HTML.

To address this problem, the Web site A List Apart has popularized a coding technique that, for obscure reasons, is named the Satay Method (after the Southeast Asian appetizer). Even Adobe has endorsed the Satay Method, but it hasn't incorporated it into Flash and Dreamweaver. If you're comfortable with HTML and you want to try it, you can find it online: go to www.alistapart .com and search for "satay."

#**77** Adjusting the Flash Publish Settings

Look Both Ways

Your choice of a Flash Player version may hinge upon which is more important: the audience or the movie's content. If the audience is more important, you'll want to find out which version of the player they're likely to have and design the movie with that version's capabilities, however limited they might be, in mind. If the content is more important—for example, if you need to use Timeline Effects or linked video files to get your point across—then your choice of a player is limited to the recent versions that support the features you need.

If you've chosen Flash and HTML as your file formats in Publish Settings, you'll see a tab for each file type at the top of the dialog box. Clicking the tabs allows you to set options for both files: The HTML options will be covered in #78; the Flash options are covered here. In both cases, we'll look only at the most significant options; you can read about the others in the Help panel.

- **Version.** Each time Flash Player has been updated, it's taken a while for the new version to catch on. To make your movie available to the largest possible audience, you may want to publish a SWF file that's compatible with earlier versions of the player. The Version menu lets you choose how far back that compatibility will go. The catch is that earlier versions of the player don't support the features in later versions of Flash—for example, if your movie uses the blending modes introduced in Flash 8, those effects will disappear if you publish your movie in Flash 7 format.

  It's best to set a target Flash Player version before you start building your movie. If you try to use a feature that isn't supported in that version, Flash gives you a warning (**Figure 77a**). However, if you go back to the Version menu and choose an earlier version of the Player *after* you've begun to develop your movie, unsupported features will disappear with no warning.

Figure 77a An alert box appears if you try to use a feature that isn't supported by the version of Flash Player that you've targeted.

- **Load order.** If a movie downloads slowly to a user's computer, this menu lets you decide in what order the layers in the Timeline will appear on the Stage. If you choose "Bottom up," the background layers load first; if you choose "Top down," the foreground layers load first. Your choice matters only if you expect members of your audience to have dial-up connections.

- **ActionScript version.** You can choose ActionScript 1.0, 2.0, or 3.0 (see #84). Early versions of the player may not support higher levels of ActionScript. ActionScript 3.0, the latest version, works in Flash Player 9 only.

- **Options.** Under most circumstances, you'll want to select these two options if the player version you've targeted supports them: "Protect from Import" stops other Flash users from importing your SWF file and using your work without permission; "Compress movie" uses lossless compression to reduce the size of the SWF file. Several of the other options that relate to debugging ActionScript will be covered in #94.

- **JPEG quality.** This slider sets default image compression quality for the movie. It doesn't override the individual settings that you made under Bitmap Properties (see #55).

- **Audio stream.** These settings are similar to those you set for event sounds in #63, but they apply to all the streaming sounds in the movie.

- **Audio event.** These settings apply to event sounds that you didn't set compression rates for in Sound Properties. If you select "Override sound settings," they'll apply to all event sounds, regardless of whether you set their compression rates individually.

#78 Adjusting the HTML Settings

Most of the settings that affect your Flash movie's appearance are contained not in the SWF file, but in the HTML file to which the SWF file is linked (see #76). Some of these settings—particularly those involving dimensions, alignment, and scale—interact in unintuitive ways.

The HTML settings are:

- **Template.** This menu allows you to choose the underlying HTML code that Flash will modify according to your settings. The default template, "Flash only," displays your Flash movie on an empty Web page, as described in #76. Most of the other templates offer minor variations for special situations.

- **Dimensions.** This menu allows you to specify the dimensions of the rectangular frame in which your movie is displayed in the Web browser window. (Flash refers to this as a *window*, but we'll call it a *frame* to distinguish it from the browser window.) The default choice is Match Movie, which means that the frame will be the same size as your movie. The other choices are Pixels, which allows you to specify exact dimensions for the frame, and Percent, which allows you to specify the frame size as a percentage of the size of the browser window, so it resizes along with the browser window.

  Note that these settings apply to the *frame*, not to the movie itself. Keeping that distinction in mind will make the alignment and scale settings easier to understand.

- **Playback.** These options control the behavior of your movie rather than its appearance. For example, the Loop option is selected by default, and you can deselect it if you want the movie to play once and stop. However, the "Loop" and "Paused at start" options are controlled much more reliably by ActionScript than by HTML. (One reason is that ActionScript commands continue to work if the SWF file is separated from the HTML file.) The "Display menu" option determines whether the user can right-click the movie to see a contextual menu, but the menu doesn't allow the user to do much besides zoom in and out.

- **Quality.** These settings control the trade-off between playback speed and image quality. The lower settings favor faster playback; the higher settings sacrifice playback speed in favor of better appearance. The default choice, High, is suitable in most situations, but the most appropriate setting will depend on the content of your movie and on the computers used by your target audience.

- **Window Mode.** Choosing Transparent Windowless from this menu causes the background of the Stage to become transparent, allowing other content on the HTML page (such as a background pattern) to show through. Because this feature doesn't work reliably in all browsers, most Flash developers stay with the default choice, Window, which leaves the movie's background opaque.

- **HTML Alignment.** This menu determines how the frame in which the movie appears is positioned in relation to the other content on the Web page.

- **Scale.** This menu works with the Dimensions options. It controls how the movie adapts to frame dimensions that are different from the size of the original movie (**Figure 78a**). "Show all" and "No border" both assure that the movie always maintains its original aspect ratio (width to height). If the aspect ratio of the frame is different from that of the movie, "Show all" adapts by using letterbox-type borders, while "No border" crops part of the movie. In contrast, "Exact fit" causes the movie to adopt the aspect ratio of the frame, even if this distorts the image. The "No scale" setting is similar to "No border," but it keeps the movie from scaling even if the size of the frame changes dynamically.

(continued on next page)

- **Flash Alignment.** This setting comes into play if the dimensions of the frame are smaller than those of the movie and Scale is set to "No border" or "No scale," causing the movie to be cropped. Flash Alignment determines which area of the movie remains visible. For example, in the "No border" illustration in **Figure 78a**, Flash Alignment is set to Top Left.

Show all

No border

Exact fit

Figure 78a The Scale settings determine how a movie adapts to a frame whose dimensions are different from those of the movie.

#79 Previewing and Publishing a Movie

Once you've adjusted the Publish Settings, you can publish your movie by clicking the Publish button at the bottom of the Publish Settings dialog box. Alternatively, you can click OK to store the settings in the FLA file, then publish the movie later by choosing File > Publish.

Flash has a Publish Preview feature, but its name is misleading: It might more accurately be called Publish *Post*view. There's no way to see what your published movie is going to look like without actually publishing it. When you choose File > Publish Preview and pick a file type (**Figure 79a**), Flash responds in the same way as it would to File > Publish—that is, it publishes the movie—but then it goes one step further: It opens the published file in a suitable application so you can look at it. If you've published an HTML file, Flash loads it into your default browser; if you've published a QuickTime file, Flash opens it in QuickTime Player. If you don't like what you see, you can modify the movie or the parameters in the Publish Settings dialog and publish it again; the new files will overwrite the old ones.

Figure 79a The choices available in the Publish Preview submenu depend on which file formats you've selected in Publish Settings.

(continued on next page)

By default, published files are saved to the same folder as the original FLA file. Assuming you've published your movie for the Web, you'll end up with at least two new files (SWF and HTML), but you may find a third file as well: a JavaScript file called AC_RunActiveContent.js. (For information on this file, see the sidebar "Active Discontent.") In addition, if your movie includes imported video, there may already be two files in the folder: an FLV file containing the video, and a SWF file containing the skin you selected for the video player (see #71). All of these files—except, of course, the FLA file—have to be uploaded to your Web server for the movie to work properly.

Active Discontent

In 2006, Microsoft made a significant change to its Internet Explorer browser. Previously, if a Web page contained ActiveX controls—a category of software that includes Flash Player, QuickTime Player, and Adobe Reader, among others—the user could interact with them immediately. The revised browser disabled these controls until the user accepted each control by clicking it. Other software developers followed Microsoft's lead and made the same change in their own browsers.

The change was made for security reasons, and although it was widely agreed to be necessary, nobody actually liked it. In preparation for the change, companies such as Apple and Adobe developed work-arounds to make browsers act the way they used to. In Adobe's case, one solution was to create a JavaScript file that could fool the browser into thinking that an ActiveX control was outside the Web page rather than embedded in it. Dreamweaver and Flash now generate this file when you save or publish a file that contains "active content." If a file called AC_RunActiveContent.js suddenly appears on your computer, don't throw it away; upload it to your Web server along with the other files you've created in Dreamweaver or Flash.

#80 Using Flash Detection

Ever since Flash came into being, its developers have grappled with the problem of how to handle users who don't have the latest version of Flash Player or who don't have the player at all. What happens when such a user comes to a Web site with Flash content?

Early versions of Flash left this problem to the individual user; later versions experimented with various ways to detect the existence and version number of the player. No form of Flash detection turned out to be foolproof. The latest implementation of Flash detection in CS3 *still* isn't foolproof—for example, it works only with Flash Player 4 and later—but it's much more reliable than earlier attempts.

To implement Flash detection:

1. In Publish Settings, select SWF and HTML as your file formats.

2. Click the Flash tab and choose the version of Flash Player that you targeted (see #77).

3. Click the HTML tab and choose a template.

4. Directly below the Template menu, select the Detect Flash Version check box.

5. In the Version field underneath, fill in the version of Flash Player that you're targeting. (The minor revision numbers are optional.)

6. Publish the movie. You'll get a SWF file, an HTML file, and an AC_RunActiveContent.js file as usual.

7. Open the HTML file in a text editor or Web-editing program, and scroll down to the line that says `var alternateContent = 'Alternate HTML content should be placed here.'` (**Figure 80a**).

(continued on next page)

```
52          'allowFullScreen','false',
53          'movie', 'myMovie',
54          'salign', ''
55       ); //end AC code
56    } else { // flash is too old or we can't detect the plugin
57       var alternateContent = 'Alternate HTML content should be placed here.'
58          + 'This content requires the Adobe Flash Player.'
59          + '<a href=http://www.macromedia.com/go/getflash/>Get Flash</a>';
60       document.write(alternateContent); // insert non-flash content
61    }
62 }
63 // -->
64 </script>
65 <noscript>
66    // Provide alternate content for browsers that do not support scripting
67    // or for those that have scripting disabled.
68    Alternate HTML content should be placed here. This content requires the Adobe
   Flash Player.
69    <a href="http://www.macromedia.com/go/getflash/">Get Flash</a>
70 </noscript>
71 </body>
72 </html>
```

Figure 80a The alternate content is highlighted in this view of the published HTML code.

There are three lines of text, each enclosed in single quotation marks and joined to the others by a plus sign. These lines of text are what will be seen by a user who has the wrong version of Flash Player, or doesn't have the player at all. By default, the text provides a link for downloading the latest version of the player, but you can substitute whatever content you want. (You can add more lines if you're careful to follow the same syntax.)

8. Scroll down further, until you get to the line that says // Provide alternate content for browsers that do not support scripting.

Below that comment, there's another copy of the alternate content that you saw in step 7 (although not in quotation marks this time). This text is what will be seen by a user whose browser has JavaScript turned off.

As before, you can leave the alternate content as it is or replace it with your own.

9. Save the file and upload it to your Web server along with the SWF file, the JavaScript file, and any other necessary files.

Your setup of Flash detection is complete. Except in rare cases, users who visit your Web page with the appropriate version of Flash Player will see your movie; others will see the alternate content (**Figure 80b**).

Figure 80b By default, users who have the wrong version of Flash Player see this text in the browser window, but you can substitute your own content.

Biological Flash Detection

If you find the Flash detection technique described here to be inelegant and unwieldy, consider a low-tech option that's worked well for years: *Let the user take care of it.* Many Web sites start with an entrance page alerting the user that "This site requires version such-and-such of Flash Player." Below, there's one link to download the player and another link to enter the site. Most of the time, the user can figure out what to do.

#81 Creating a Projector

A *projector* is a hybrid executable file (or application) that combines a SWF file and Flash Player. Regardless of whether the viewer's computer has Flash Player installed, double-clicking a projector causes the embedded movie to play.

To create a projector, select Windows Projector or Macintosh Projector on the Formats tab in the Publish Settings dialog box. (The Windows version won't work on a Mac, nor vice versa.) No extra tabs appear, and there are no options to select. When you publish the movie, the projector appears in the same folder as the FLA file.

Because most computers have Flash Player installed, projectors aren't needed very often. Their large file size (at least 2 MB for Windows, and nearly 10 MB for Mac) makes them unsuitable for use on the Web. They're most often used for distributing Flash movies on CD-ROM.

Projectors become more useful when they're combined with Action-Script. Many people who aren't professional programmers use Flash as a tool for developing applications: They do the programming in Action-Script and output the result as a projector. Just as double-clicking the Flash icon launches Flash, double-clicking a projector icon initiates whatever the projector has been programmed to do, even if that has nothing to do with animation (**Figure 81a**).

Figure 81a This desktop clock/timer was built in Flash, programmed in ActionScript, and published as a projector.

#82 Publishing a QuickTime Movie

Flash can output two kinds of QuickTime files. A traditional QuickTime file, in which Flash animation and sound are converted to standard video and audio tracks, is available through File > Export > Export Movie. This type of file is appropriate for burning to a DVD or importing to a video-editing program.

In Publish Settings, a newer type of format is available: a QuickTime file with a Flash track that's essentially an embedded SWF file. The Flash track doesn't support features beyond Flash 5, but all the distinctive features of a SWF file are preserved, including scalable vector paths, streaming sounds, and interactivity (**Figure 82a**).

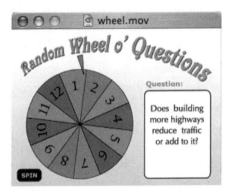

Figure 82a All the properties of a SWF file are preserved when it's converted to a Flash track in a QuickTime file. The QuickTime movie shown here has no video or audio track, just a Flash track.

Follow these steps to publish a movie in QuickTime format.

1. In Publish Settings, select "Flash (.swf)," "HTML (.html)," and "QuickTime with Flash track" as your file formats.

2. Click the Flash tab and choose Flash Player 5 from the Version menu. Modify the other settings as needed, just as you would for an ordinary SWF file (see #77).

3. To include the QuickTime file in a Web page, click the HTML tab and choose QuickTime from the Template menu. Leave the other settings alone; they have no effect when you publish a QuickTime file.

(continued on next page)

4. Click the QuickTime tab and adjust any or all of the following settings:

- **Dimensions.** You can select Match Movie or fill in custom dimensions in pixels.

- **Alpha; Layers.** These menus affect how the Flash track interacts with other visible tracks in the QuickTime file. When you publish the movie in Flash, there are no other visible tracks, but you can add tracks later—video, text, or graphics, for example—in an editing program such as QuickTime Pro.

- **Streaming sound.** If "Use QuickTime compression" is selected, all the sounds in your Flash movie are mixed into a single QuickTime audio track with attributes that you can set, such as compression and bit rate. If it's not selected, the sounds remain part of the Flash track.

- **Controller.** You can decide whether you want the user to have control over playing, stopping, and rewinding the movie.

- **Playback.** "Loop" and "Paused at start" are identical to the similarly named options on the HTML tab. "Play every frame" mutes the sound so that QuickTime Player does not have to skip frames to keep the video in sync with the audio.

- **File.** If "Flatten (Make self-contained)" is selected, the Flash track is embedded in the QuickTime file. If it isn't selected, the QuickTime file is linked to an external SWF file that must be present for the Flash content to play.

5. Click Publish to publish the movie or OK to save the settings.

#**83** Exporting Still Images

Standard Web browsers can display images in the JPEG, GIF, and PNG formats, but unlike GIFs, JPEG and PNG files can't contain animation. If you save your movie as JPEG or PNG, the resulting file will contain only the frame at which the playhead is positioned at the time you export.

Although Flash offers the choice of exporting or publishing, single frames often look better when exported than when published. For example, publishing GIF or PNG files with transparent backgrounds doesn't work properly, but exporting the same images is problem-free.

The ability to export a single frame is handy if you want to include portions of your animation in printed material. Also, it allows you to substitute a still image for an animation in Web browsers that don't have the Flash plug-in (see #80).

Each file format has different strengths and weaknesses:

- **GIF.** As noted in #75, GIF has trouble with continuous-tone images; it's better suited to technical or cartoon-style drawings that have sharp edges and areas of flat color. Unlike JPEG, however, GIF supports transparency: If you select the Transparent option, the background color of the Stage drops out.

- **JPEG.** As you saw in #55, JPEG compression can store full-color images in amazingly small files. Apart from that, however, the JPEG file format doesn't have much going for it: It doesn't hold color very accurately, and anything more than moderate compression introduces obvious artifacts.

- **PNG.** PNG is a robust, multipurpose format that combines the best aspects of all the others: It supports full color, masking, and transparency, and it's capable of very good compression. Unfortunately, support for its features is still spotty: Flash doesn't implement compression in PNG files, and some browsers still don't support PNG transparency.

(continued on next page)

Although the JPEG and PNG file formats don't support multiple frames, as GIF does, it is possible to export a Flash movie as an *image sequence*, in which all the movie frames are saved as a series of serially numbered files in the bitmap format of your choice. (**Figure 83a**). You'll find this option under Export > Export Movie (not, as you might guess, under Export Image). Image sequences are especially useful when you want to enhance each frame individually in Photoshop and then reassemble the movie. Many video-editing programs, including Adobe Premiere Pro, recognize image sequences and import them as continuous video clips.

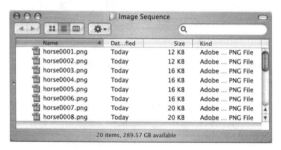

Figure 83a When you export an image sequence, each frame is saved to an individual file.

CHAPTER TEN

Using Basic ActionScript

Using Flash can be like visiting a restaurant in a foreign country. To request a standard meal, you can point to what you want on the menu. But to get something prepared a special way, you have to talk to the waiter—and to do that, you have to speak the waiter's language.

The language Flash understands is ActionScript. If you can "speak" in ActionScript, you can get Flash to do almost anything you want.

Like any other language, ActionScript requires serious study and practice: Reading a task-based book like this isn't enough. This chapter presents just a taste of how ActionScript works and what its capabilities are. To learn underlying principles and more techniques, read a more in-depth ActionScript book such as *Flash CS3 Professional Advanced for Windows and Macintosh: Visual QuickPro Guide* by Russell Chun.

In the meantime, you can learn a few phrases to use in a pinch—the Flash equivalent of being able to say "Diet Coke, no ice" in a way that the waiter will understand.

#84 Choosing an Appropriate ActionScript Version

The original version of ActionScript—now known as ActionScript 1.0—was designed to be easy for beginners to use. At the time, no one envisioned that Flash would become a professional-level tool for building complex interfaces and Web applications. As more serious programmers began to use Flash, they became frustrated with ActionScript's limitations. Macromedia responded with ActionScript 2.0, which gave ActionScript many of the capabilities available in object-oriented programming languages such as C++.

ActionScript 3.0, the first version to be released by Adobe, is a complete rewrite of ActionScript. Not only are the structure and syntax significantly different from those in ActionScript 1.0, but ActionScript 3.0's technical underpinnings have changed so radically that it's no longer compatible with its predecessors. Flash Player 9 is essentially two players combined: one to execute ActionScript 3.0 and one to execute earlier versions.

The continued existence of that virtual "second player" is good news. For the time being, Flash allows you to use whichever version of ActionScript you're most comfortable with. For beginners, that's usually ActionScript 1.0, perhaps with a few techniques from 2.0 thrown in. Because ActionScript 3.0 is aimed at experienced programmers, we won't be working with it very much in this chapter. (You'll get a better look at 3.0 in Chapter 11.)

When you create a new document, the first decision Flash requires you to make is whether you want it to use ActionScript 2.0 or 3.0; choosing 2.0 allows you to use 1.0 as well. The choice you make determines which versions of Flash Player you can target in Publish Settings (see #77) and which commands are available to you in the Actions panel (see #85). Once you've made that decision for a particular FLA file, it can't be changed (**Figure 84a**).

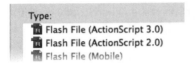

Figure 84a There's no such thing as a generic FLA file anymore. When you select File > New, you must choose between ActionScript 2.0 and 3.0.

The scripting techniques you'll learn in this chapter are labeled with the version of ActionScript to which they apply. If you want to try them out, be sure to do so in a FLA file that's been set for the appropriate version; they won't work otherwise.

#85 Using the Actions Panel

The Actions panel is where you write and edit ActionScript code. To open it, choose Window > Actions or press F9 (Windows) or Option-F9 (Mac). If you've selected an instance of a movie clip or button symbol on the Stage (in ActionScript 1.0/2.0) or a keyframe in the Timeline (all versions), you can open the Actions panel by clicking the ActionScript icon in the Property inspector (**Figure 85a**).

ActionScript

Figure 85a This icon appears in the Property inspector when you've selected a keyframe or a symbol instance to which a script can be attached. Click the icon to open the Actions panel.

By default, the Actions panel has three panes, although it can acquire a fourth if you turn on Script Assist (see #86). The top-left pane, called the Actions toolbox, contains a categorized list of the elements used in the version of ActionScript that you selected, including commands, functions, classes, methods, properties, and other elements (**Figure 85b**). The right pane, called the Script pane, is where you write and edit your scripts. Double-clicking an ActionScript element in the toolbox causes it to appear in the Script pane, accompanied by any necessary punctuation.

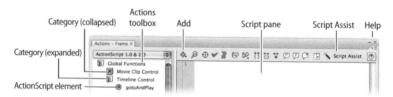

Figure 85b In the Actions panel, categories are indicated by an open or closed book icon; ActionScript elements are indicated by a round ActionScript icon.

Most beginners prefer to look up the ActionScript elements they need in the toolbox and double-click them to let Flash "write" a script in the Script pane, usually with the aid of Script Assist. If you're not sure what an item means or how it's used, you can select it and click the Help icon for an explanation.

If you prefer, you can choose ActionScript elements from menus and submenus by clicking the Add icon, but you can't use Help in that case.

Tip

Another way to add an element to your script is to drag it directly from the toolbox into the Script pane.

Once you have enough experience with ActionScript, you can choose to type your code directly into the Script pane—which is much faster but can lead to mistakes.

If you have more than one script in your FLA file, the bottom-left pane—called the Script navigator—helps you find the one you're looking for. Double-clicking a script in the Script navigator "pins" the script, keeping it visible in the Actions panel even if you select something else on the Stage or in the Timeline.

#86 Using Script Assist

Arguments About Parameters

In reference material about ActionScript, you may see parameters referred to as *arguments*. Technically, a *parameter* is the type of information a command requires (for example, getURL requires a URL), and an *argument* is the value supplied for that parameter (for example, http://www.adobe.com/). Many writers don't make that distinction, however, so you'll often see the two terms used interchangeably. Adobe's documentation uses "parameters" to mean both, so we've done the same in this book.

Most ActionScript commands require additional information in order for Flash to carry them out. For example, if you use the ActionScript 1.0 command getURL (which opens a Web link), Flash has to know which URL you want it to click and in which browser window you want the Web page to open. These extra pieces of information are called parameters.

If you're not experienced with ActionScript, you probably don't know what parameters a particular command requires and how they need to be coded. Clicking the Script Assist button (see **Figure 85b**) opens a new pane in the Actions panel that helps answer these questions.

Script Assist does two things: If you select an ActionScript element in the toolbox, the Script Assist pane displays a brief description of that element (**Figure 86a**). If you bring that element into the Script pane by double-clicking or dragging it, Script Assist adds a field or menu for each parameter that the command requires. As you fill in each parameter, Script Assist adds it to the script with the proper syntax.

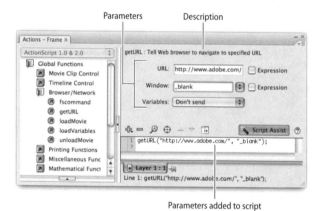

Figure 86a The Script Assist pane defines the selected ActionScript element and provides a convenient way to specify parameters.

Good Behavior

How would you like Flash to write a whole script for you? Flash provides that service through its Behaviors feature in ActionScript 1.0 and 2.0.

Open the Behaviors panel (Window > Behaviors) and click the Add icon to see a menu of categories. Within each category, you'll find an assortment of pre-written scripts, or *behaviors,* to accomplish various tasks. When you choose one, Flash displays a dialog box in which you enter the parameters and click OK. Flash lists your chosen behavior in the Behaviors panel; in addition, if the Actions panel is open, Flash loads the script into the Script pane for you to view or edit.

Using behaviors is far from a no-brainer; you still have to give instance names to the objects you want to control (see #90), and you must understand each behavior well enough to know how to apply it. In most cases, if you know how to use a behavior effectively, you know enough to write the ActionScript yourself. For these reasons, many people use behaviors not for practical tasks, but as a learning tool: Examining these "canned" scripts and seeing how they work is a great way to become familiar with ActionScript.

#87 Writing Simple Frame Scripts (ActionScript 1.0)

ActionScript 1.0 supports two basic kinds of scripts: *Object scripts*, which will be covered in #88, are attached to objects such as buttons and movie clips. *Frame scripts*, which are covered here, are attached to keyframes in the Timeline.

Every script is associated with an *event* that acts as a trigger: Something happens—either initiated by the user or by Flash itself—that causes the commands in the script to be executed. In the case of a frame script, that event is the playhead's arrival at the keyframe to which the script is attached.

For a very simple example, suppose you have a movie that's 20 frames long. When the playhead leaves frame 20, its default behavior is to snap back to frame 1, causing the movie to loop. In this case, however, you want the movie to play once and stop.

You can accomplish this with a frame script:

1. Insert a keyframe in frame 20.

2. With that keyframe selected, go to the Actions panel and make sure that the script type at the upper-left corner is "Actions - Frame" (**Figure 87a**). If it's anything other than that, the keyframe isn't selected. Go back and reselect it.

Figure 87a When you create your "stop" script, the Actions panel should look like this.

3. In the Actions toolbox, choose Global Functions > Timeline Control > stop.

4. Double-click "stop" or drag it into the Script pane. It now appears like this:

```
stop();
```

For an explanation of the odd punctuation, see the sidebar "Syntax, Part 1."

Note

When you write a script in the Actions panel, you don't have to press Enter or click an OK button to make the script "stick." A script becomes active the moment it's entered in the Script pane.

5. Preview or test the movie. When the playhead reaches frame 20, it executes the script and the movie stops.

You can tell that a keyframe has a frame script attached to it by the letter *a* that appears in the Timeline (**Figure 87b**). Technically, you can attach a script to any keyframe. In practice, however, it's highly recommended that you add a new layer and put *all* your frame scripts in that layer. (Most people call the layer "Actions" or "Scripts," and they put it at the top of the Timeline so it can be seen easily.)

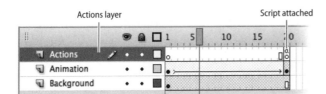

Figure 87b Frame scripts (indicated by the letter *a*) should be placed in a layer of their own.

Besides stop, the command used most frequently in simple frame scripts is "go to." For example, imagine a 20-frame animation in which a match lights a candle and exits in frame 15, leaving the candle flame flickering. You'd want the candle-lighting portion of the animation to play

(continued on next page)

Syntax, Part 1

Every ActionScript command or function is followed by a set of parentheses intended to hold parameters. For example, in gotoAndPlay(16), the parameter is the frame number 16. Some commands, such as stop(), don't require parameters, but the parentheses still must be there.

Many scripts have multiple commands that are executed in sequence. We tell Flash where each command ends by putting a semicolon after it. Even in a script that consists of only one command, the semicolon is still needed:

stop();

once, but you'd want the candle to go on flickering indefinitely. In that case, you could attach a script to frame 20 that tells the playhead to jump to frame 16. The technique is illustrated in **Figure 87c**.

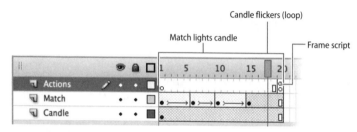

Figure 87c Every time the playhead reaches frame 20, a frame script causes the playhead to go to frame 16.

#**88** Writing Simple Button Scripts (ActionScript 1.0)

In #27, you created a button symbol that responded to mouse input but didn't do anything else. To make an instance of the button functional, you have to attach a script to it. (For easier reading, we'll refer to an instance of a button symbol simply as a "button.")

Object scripts, such as those attached to a button, differ from frame scripts in one important respect: The user, not Flash, initiates the events that trigger them. As you remember from #87, the only event that can trigger a frame script is the playhead's arrival at the frame to which the script is attached. In contrast, a script attached to a button can be triggered by any number of events. For example, when a user's pointer is over a button on the Stage, the user might press the mouse button; release the mouse button; press the mouse button and roll away from the button symbol, then release the mouse button; and so on (you get the idea).

Unlike a frame script, an object script must not only contain a set of commands, but it must also specify the event that will cause those commands to be executed. An event is preceded by the keyword *on,* as in on (release).

Imagine that you've placed a button on the Stage that you want the viewer to use to pause the movie. You could do it this way:

1. Select the button on the Stage.

2. Go to the Actions panel and make sure that the script type at the upper-left corner is "Actions - Button" (**Figure 88a**). If it's anything other than that, the button isn't selected. Go back and reselect it.

3. If the Actions panel doesn't include the Script Assist pane, click the Script Assist button to make it appear.

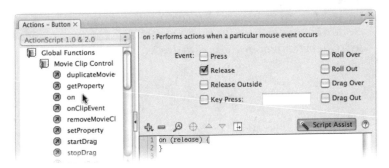

Figure 88a When you write a button script, the Actions panel looks like this.

(continued on next page)

208

Syntax, Part 2

ActionScript uses braces to identify commands that will be executed if a condition is met or a specified event takes place. This illustrates the general structure:

```
if (this is true) {do
this};
```

The ActionScript could be written on one line as above, but that arrangement makes it difficult to read—especially if there are multiple commands. The convention is to insert line breaks after the first brace and before the last, and to indent the commands between the braces, like so:

```
on (release) {
  stop();
}
```

Flash ignores line breaks, tabs, and extra spaces when it interprets ActionScript.

4. In the Actions toolbox, choose Global Functions > Movie Clip Control > on.

5. Double-click "on" or drag it into the Script pane.

6. In the Script Assist pane, choose the event that will trigger the script. For button scripts, that event is usually "release." (The user-interface convention is for a button click to take effect when the user releases the mouse button.)

 The Script pane now shows:

```
on (release) {
}
```

 See the sidebar "Syntax, Part 2" for an explanation of the placement of the braces.

7. Choose Global Functions > Timeline Control > stop.

8. Double-click "stop" or drag it to line 1 in the Script pane. The script now looks like this:

```
on (release) {
  stop();
}
```

9. Preview or test the movie. When you click the pause button, the movie stops.

 To allow the user to resume the movie, you can create a play button: Follow the same steps, but choose "play" rather than "stop" in step 7.

Note

Unlike frame scripts, object scripts don't show up in the Timeline. If you create a button script and the letter a *appears in a keyframe, you didn't select the button properly. Go back to step 2.*

#89 Organizing the Timeline for Interactivity

When you play an audio CD, you can listen to it all the way through from beginning to end, or you can jump from one track to another. The Flash Timeline can work the same way. The techniques we've worked with so far involve playing the Timeline continuously from beginning to end, but it's also possible to divide it into discrete segments and let the user decide which to play.

For example, imagine a Flash movie that shows a neutral face and two buttons, one labeled Happy and one labeled Sad. If the user clicks the Happy button, you want the corners of the mouth to turn upward; if the user clicks the Sad button, you want them to turn downward (**Figure 89a**).

Figure 89a The static frame at the beginning of the movie is shown on the left. In the center, you see the result of clicking the Happy button; on the right, the result of clicking the Sad button.

You can accomplish this task by dividing the Timeline into three segments. The first segment displays the neutral face; since it's not animated, it only has to be one frame long. The second segment animates the transition from neutral to happy; the third segment animates the transition from neutral to sad (**Figure 89b**).

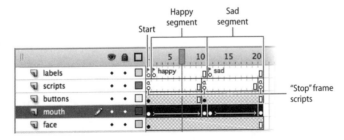

Figure 89b The Timeline has been divided into three segments, each of which begins with a frame label and ends with a "stop" frame script.

(continued on next page)

To make this arrangement work, you need button scripts and frame scripts. Assuming that the "happy" segment of the Timeline starts at frame 2 and the "sad" segment starts at frame 12, you'd attach the following script to the Happy button:

```
on (release) {
    gotoAndPlay (2);
}
```

You'd attach a similar script to the Sad button, but with 12 as the frame number. (To attach a script to a button, see #88; to use the "go to" command, see #87.)

All that's left is to add some "stop" frame scripts: one in frame 1, to keep the playhead from moving until the user clicks a button; one in frame 11, to stop the playhead from moving into the "sad" segment when it comes to the end of the "happy" segment; and one in the final frame, to prevent the playhead from snapping back to frame 1.

There's one problem with this arrangement: If you move any of the keyframes to lengthen or shorten the animation, you'll have to change the frame numbers in the scripts. If you forget to do that, or if you change the numbers incorrectly, the movie won't work.

The solution to this problem is to add *frame labels* to the beginning of each segment. To do this, insert a keyframe (if there's not one there already), select the keyframe, and type a label into the Frame field in the Property inspector (**Figure 89c**). The label appears in the Timeline, marked by a red flag.

Note

Since your frame labels are being used in scripts, it's important that they follow standard ActionScript naming rules: Each label should begin with a lowercase letter and contain only letters and numbers, with no spaces or punctuation.

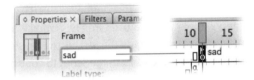

Figure 89c Entering a frame label in the Property inspector (left) makes the label appear in the Timeline (right).

You can now change the frame numbers in the script parameters to frame labels, as in:

```
on (release) {
    gotoAndPlay ("happy");
}
```

The frame label has to be in quotation marks; also, ActionScript is case-sensitive, so you can't use "Happy" as the parameter if the frame label is "happy."

Like frame scripts, frame labels are best placed in a layer of their own at the top of the Timeline. If you need to move a keyframe of animation, you can select the frame label at the same time and move them in tandem.

#90
Controlling Objects from a Frame Script (ActionScript 2.0)

Attaching scripts to objects on the Stage in ActionScript 1.0 is intuitive and convenient, but it presents a problem: If you want to review or edit all the scripts in a movie, you don't always know where to find them.

Since the introduction of ActionScript 2.0, the recommended practice has been to move all of a movie's object scripts into a single frame script. (In ActionScript 3.0, attaching scripts to objects is no longer allowed.)

Let's work with the same example that we used in #89: a movie in which the Happy button causes a face to smile and the Sad button causes it to frown. In this case, however, we want to use a frame script to control the buttons.

Before ActionScript can send a command to an object, it has to know which object it's talking to. Therefore, each button has to be given a unique *instance name*. You assign an instance name to an object the same way you assign a label to a keyframe: Select it and type a name in the Instance Name field in the Property inspector (**Figure 90a**). For this example, give the Happy button the instance name happy_btn and the Sad button the instance name sad_btn.

Note
An instance name must begin with a lowercase letter and contain only letters and numbers, with no spaces or punctuation. The "_btn" suffix isn't required, but it's recommended for button instances, as is the "_mc" suffix for movie-clip instances.

Figure 90a Select an object and type its name in the Instance Name field of the Property inspector. Only instances of buttons and movie clips can be given instance names.

Objects are typically controlled from a frame script in frame 1. In this case, frame 1 already contains a frame script with the stop command. To edit the script, select its keyframe in the Timeline. The script appears in the Script pane of the Actions panel.

Here's how to add the necessary commands to the frame script:

1. If the Script Assist pane is visible, click the Script Assist button to eliminate it. (Script Assist works well for simple scripts, but not for the more advanced technique we're using here.)

2. Click the first blank line in the Script pane. If there is no blank line, click at the end of the script and press Enter (Windows) or Return (Mac) to create one.

3. Click the Insert Target Path icon (**Figure 90b**). A dialog box appears, listing all of the objects with instance names.

Figure 90b Clicking the Insert Target Path icon opens a dialog box that lists all of the objects with instance names.

4. Select happy_btn and click OK. The Script pane displays `this.happy_btn` followed by a flashing cursor.

5. Press the Period key. (In ActionScript, a command and its targeted instance are separated by a period, usually referred to as a *dot*.) A list box appears, containing all the possible ActionScript elements that might follow the instance name.

6. Scroll down the list and double-click "onRelease." The onRelease event appears after the dot in the Script pane.

7. Complete the script by typing the code shown in bold:

```
stop();
this.happy_btn.onRelease = function() {
  gotoAndPlay("happy");
}
```

(continued on next page)

Loosely speaking, a *function* is a piece of code that accepts an input and delivers an output. In this case, you've created a function that accepts a mouse-release event from happy_btn and outputs a "go to" command.

8. Select the Happy button on the Stage. Its attached object script appears in the Script pane of the Actions panel.

9. Select all the text in the script and press Delete to remove it.

10. Test the movie. It should work identically to the movie in #89.

You can now follow the same series of steps for the Sad button, substituting "sad" for "happy" as needed.

#91 Converting Animation to ActionScript (ActionScript 3.0)

One of the trickier parts of using ActionScript is coding an object's movement on the Stage. A series of motion tweens that takes a few minutes to create in the Timeline could take hours to re-create in ActionScript.

Why would you *want* to animate objects in ActionScript rather than in the Timeline? Usually, it's because you want to vary the animation while the movie is playing—for example, by giving the user controls that allow the movement to be sped up, slowed down, or redirected. If the animation is coded as a function in ActionScript, you can change any aspect of the animation by feeding new parameters to the function.

Flash CS3 has the ability to convert Timeline animation to ActionScript code. It works with motion tweens only—not with shape tweens or frame-by-frame animation—and it converts to ActionScript 3.0 only. To use it:

1. Motion-tween an object on the Stage. The animation can be as elaborate as you want: It can contain any number of intermediate keyframes, and it can even use a motion guide (see #40).

2. Choose a movie-clip symbol to which you want to copy the animation and drag an instance to the Stage. (Graphic and button symbols won't work.)

3. Give the new object an instance name (see #90).

4. In the Timeline, select all the frames of the original object's motion tween (**Figure 91a**).

Figure 91a The animation you copy can have as many keyframes as you want, as long as they are confined to one layer.

5. Choose Edit > Timeline > Copy Motion as ActionScript 3.0. A dialog box appears, asking for the instance name of the object to which you want to apply the animation.

(continued on next page)

6. Type the instance name from step 3 and click OK.

7. If there's not already an Actions layer in the Timeline, create one; then select the keyframe in frame 1.

8. Open the Actions panel (if it's not already open) and click in the Script pane.

9. Choose Edit > Paste. The ActionScript code representing the animation appears in the pane.

10. Test the movie and compare the coded motion of the second object to the Timeline animation of the first object. They should look the same.

Try changing some parameters in the ActionScript code, then test the movie again. The coded animation will look different; the Timeline animation will stay the same.

If you wish, you can remove the original object from the Timeline.

#92 Using External AS Files (ActionScript 2.0 and 3.0)

The scripts we've worked with so far have all been embedded in the FLA file. You have the option, however, of keeping your scripts in external files. External files are useful for editing scripts without having to open them in Flash, storing scripts that are too long to fit conveniently into the Actions panel, or sharing one script among several movies.

An external script file is a plain text file. You can create one in any text-editing program, as long as you save it with the filename extension .as. Another option is to use the Script window built into Flash. Like the Actions panel, it contains an Actions toolbox and other tools to help you write and edit your script (**Figure 92a**). When you save a script in the Script window, the resulting file is automatically given the .as extension.

Show/Hide Toolbox

Figure 92a The Script window initially appears with the Actions toolbox hidden. To access the toolbox, click the Show/Hide Toolbox icon.

The Script window is often overlooked because it's not on the Window menu—or, for that matter, any other menu. To get to it, choose File > New to open the New File dialog box, then choose ActionScript File from the list of file types. To edit an existing AS file in the Script window, double-click the file outside of Flash or choose File > Open in Flash.

An AS file won't be executed unless you associate it with a specific FLA file:

1. Put the AS file and the FLA file in the same folder.

2. Add a frame script or edit the existing frame script in frame 1 of the FLA file's Timeline. Add the command include "*filename*.as" (keeping the quotation marks, but replacing *filename* with the actual name of the file).

3. Test or publish the movie. Flash incorporates the contents of the AS file into the SWF file.

(continued on next page)

Because the AS file is needed only when you create the SWF file—not when you play it—there's no need to upload AS files to a Web server. However, if you make any changes to the AS file, they won't take effect until you generate a new SWF file.

Note

Some types of ActionScript code, such as definitions of classes, must be in external files. To associate those with a FLA file, you use the import *command rather than* include.

#93 Formatting and Validating a Script

As we noted in #88, Flash ignores tabs, line breaks, and extra spaces when it interprets ActionScript. An entire script could be written on one long line, and Flash wouldn't know the difference: It pays attention only to punctuation such as parentheses, braces, and semicolons.

Nevertheless, it's important to format a script neatly and consistently, so that people who edit your script can know at a glance what's going on. Flash does some formatting on the fly when you type in the Actions panel or Script window, but it doesn't do really thorough formatting until you click the "Auto format" icon (**Figure 93a**).

Check syntax   Auto format

Figure 93a These icons appear in the Actions panel only if Script Assist is turned off.

In order to format your script, Flash has to *understand* the script: It has to know which words are commands, which are variables, which are properties, and so on. Assuming your spelling, syntax, and punctuation are correct, Flash has no trouble figuring out what's what. If you've made even a single error, however, Flash loses its bearings. As a result, when you click "Auto format," you may see an alert telling you that formatting was unsuccessful (**Figure 93b**).

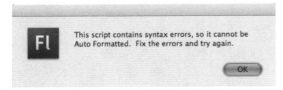

Figure 93b This alert appears if errors in your script prevent Flash from formatting it.

(continued on next page)

Finding a mistake can be difficult when there's only one incorrect character among thousands. Flash makes the task easier by giving you some guidance: A panel called Compiler Errors pops up and lists the errors that Flash found (**Figure 93c**).

Figure 93c The Compiler Errors panel describes the problems Flash found in your script.

Note
Clicking the "Check syntax" icon finds and identifies the same errors that clicking "Auto format" does, but without attempting to format your script.

#94 Testing an Interactive Movie

The "Check syntax" and "Auto format" features find errors in the *structure* of your script, but they don't find errors in the content. Suppose you have the following script in frame 1:

```
this.myButton_btn.onRelease = function() {
    myInstance_mc._visible = false;
}
```

When the user clicks the button called myButton_btn, this script is supposed to cause a movie-clip instance called myInstance_mc to become invisible. In the Actions panel, the script checks out with no errors; the vocabulary and syntax are fine.

But when you test the movie, it doesn't work. No matter how many times you click the button, myInstance_mc remains visible on the Stage. What do you do now?

First you need to figure out where the problems lie. Is the button receiving your mouse clicks? Is the frame script communicating properly with the button? Perhaps there's something wrong with myInstance_mc?

Next you need to test each of these possibilities. In a situation like this, the *trace* command is indispensable; its job is to send you status reports from inside a movie.

For example, you might modify your frame script like so:

```
this.myButton_btn.onRelease = function() {
    trace ("The button has been clicked");
}
```

The trace command communicates through a panel called Output. In this case, when you test the movie and click the button, the Output panel pops open and displays the message "The button has been clicked." This tells you that the button is receiving your mouse clicks and that the frame script is working.

The trace command can send two types of messages. The first is what's called a *string*—a collection of characters that ActionScript doesn't understand, but you do. A string is surrounded by quotation marks. When the trace command is executed, it simply repeats what's between the quotation marks—in this case, "The button has been clicked."

(continued on next page)

The other type of message trace can send is a *value*. For example, you might modify your script to look like this:

```
this.myButton_btn.onRelease = function() {
    myInstance_mc._visible = false;
    trace (myInstance_mc._visible);
}
```

This version of the script once again tries to make the movie clip instance invisible, but that attempt is followed by a report from the trace command on the value of myInstance_mc._visible—which should, if the script is working correctly, be false.

Let's say you test the movie and click the button. On the Stage, myInstance_mc remains visible, but the Output panel displays "undefined" instead of "true." An instance has to be either visible or invisible. How can it be undefined?

This message tells you that the instance called myInstance_mc doesn't exist. How can this be? After all, you can see it on the Stage. Perhaps its instance name doesn't actually match what's in the script. For example, if you accidentally named the instance myIntance_mc, then there *is* no object called myInstance_mc.

To troubleshoot an interactive movie, you have to be part plumber, part Sherlock Holmes, and part gunslinger with the trace command in your holster.

#95 Using the Debugger

The Debugger is a panel (or, in some cases, a collection of panels) that helps you find errors in ActionScript code. Using the Debugger for the simple scripts we've discussed here is like using a sledgehammer to swat flies. For tracking down errors in a beginner's ActionScript file, the *trace* command (see #94) is usually all you need.

Most of the Debugger's features become useful with scripts that contain variables, nested functions, and if/else statements, all of which are beyond the scope of this book. However, it does have a feature that can come in handy for scripts of any size: the ability to set breakpoints.

A *breakpoint* is a pause that you insert between lines of ActionScript code. When you play a movie in the Debugger, the script stops executing at each breakpoint and continues only when you ask it to. By seeing how your script executes step by step, you can often find out where the problems are. Although ActionScript 2.0 and 3.0 use different versions of the Debugger, the breakpoint feature is the same in both.

You can add breakpoints to a script in the Actions panel by clicking in the margin to the left of any line of code. Clicking once turns a breakpoint on (identified by a red dot); clicking again turns the breakpoint off (**Figure 95a**). Breakpoints are saved with the FLA file, but they don't have any effect unless the movie is played in the Debugger.

Breakpoint

Figure 95a A breakpoint is indicated by a red dot in the left margin of a script. You can set breakpoints in the Actions panel or in the Code View pane of the Debugger.

To see your breakpoints in action, select Debug > Debug Movie. Your movie previews in Flash Player as it normally does when you test a movie, and the Debugger opens at the same time. In the Code View pane, you can see your script as it appears in the Actions panel. A yellow arrow moves from line to line as the script executes (**Figure 95b**). When it gets to a breakpoint, the execution stops.

(continued on next page)

From the breakpoint, you can step through each line of code by clicking the Step In icon, or you can click Continue to resume execution of the script. Other panes of the Debugger are constantly updated with the values of variables and objects' properties.

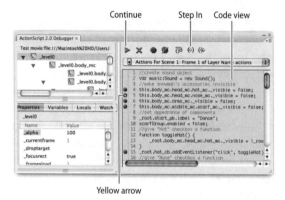

Figure 95b This is the ActionScript 2.0 Debugger. The 3.0 Debugger is laid out differently but has many of the same features.

CHAPTER ELEVEN

Using Components with ActionScript 3.0

As you work with Flash, you'll probably want to use symbols and scripts similar to ones you've used before. In those cases, it makes sense to recycle the older elements rather than re-creating them from scratch.

Flash takes that principle a step further: It provides ready-made, pre-scripted symbols called *components* that you can use in any movie. You can find them in the Components panel (Window > Components).

The ActionScript inside these components is thorough and robust, so you can depend on them to work properly. In addition, the ActionScript is already *compiled,* or translated into the "machine language" that computers understand. The downside is that you can't edit or view the components' ActionScript, but the upside is that the scripts run much faster and make fewer demands on the computer than scripts you'd write yourself.

To make the best use of components, you have to write scripts to integrate them into your movie. This chapter provides a few examples that will show you how to use components in simple ways. ActionScript reference books such as the one mentioned in Chapter 10 will help when you're ready to progress to more complex scripts.

Because ActionScript 3.0 and 2.0 can't be used in the same movie, Flash CS3 comes with two different sets of components. If you choose ActionScript 3.0 as the scripting language for a document (see #84), the Components panel shows the ActionScript 3.0 components; otherwise, it shows the ActionScript 2.0 components. The ActionScript 3.0 components are much improved over earlier versions; they're faster, lighter, and easier to use. For that reason, we'll focus on the ActionScript 3.0 components, although some of the techniques you'll see here will apply to earlier component versions as well.

#96 Getting to Know ActionScript 3.0 Components

The ActionScript 3.0 components fall into two categories: user interface (UI) and video. The UI components (**Figure 96a**) allow users to interact with programs and Web sites; they include familiar elements such as buttons, menus, sliders, check boxes, and so on. The video components (**Figure 96b**) allow users to control video that's playing back as part of a Flash movie.

Figure 96a The Components panel shown here displays ActionScript 3.0 UI components.

Figure 96b ActionScript 3.0 video components require familiarity with ActionScript—with the exception of FLVPlayback, which Flash deploys as part of the video import process.

To add an instance of a component to your movie, drag it from the Components panel onto the Stage. Two items are added to the Library: the component itself and a folder of supporting files called Component Assets. To use additional instances of the same component, drag them from the Library, not from the Components panel.

Note
If you use more than one type of component in a movie, only the first will add the Component Assets folder to the Library. Additional components will share the same set of supporting files.

Adding a component instance to your movie presents the same problem as adding a button (see #27): The component functions properly—a check box can be selected, a slider moves sideways, and so on—but it doesn't accomplish anything. To make a component useful, you have to add ActionScript code that monitors each instance of the component and responds to changes (see #100).

Please, Sir, I Want Some More

If the components that came with Flash aren't enough to satisfy you, you can get more: In Flash, choose Help > Flash Exchange, and your Web browser will take you to the home page for Adobe Exchange. Formerly a place where users could upload and download extensions for Flash, Fireworks, and Dreamweaver, the Exchange has expanded to include tutorials, clip art, filters, and other downloadable accessories for all of the products in the Creative Suite. Choosing Flash on the Exchange home page takes you to the Flash Exchange, where you'll find a variety of components and other files that you can try, buy, or use for free. Clicking the name of a file takes you to an information-and-download page.

Although there's a Category menu at the top, Components isn't one of the categories; the files are classified by function rather than by type. If you want a Flash component, click Advanced Search in the upper-right corner; then type "component" as your keyword and choose Flash as the exchange to search.

Pay attention to the version of Flash that the component is intended for: If it's Flash 8 or earlier, the component will work only in ActionScript 2.0 documents. Also be aware that most of the add-ons in the Adobe Exchange aren't supported by Adobe, so you use them at your own risk.

#97 Customizing Component Instances

While using off-the-shelf components is convenient, it's not as creatively satisfying as designing your own symbols. Flash addresses this issue by providing several ways to modify the appearance of ActionScript 3.0 components:

- **Use the Property inspector.** As with standard movie clips, you can use the buttons on the right side of the Property inspector to change the color or blending mode of a component instance. The drawback is that there's no live preview: The only way to see what your changes look like is to test or publish the movie. To get around this, go to the Instance Behavior menu (**Figure 97a**) and change the symbol type from Movie Clip to Button. (The instance may temporarily look different, but that's OK.) Make whatever changes you want to the color and blending modes, then change the symbol type back to Movie Clip.

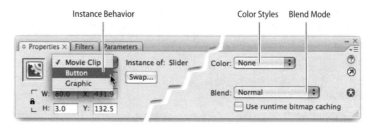

Figure 97a To allow a live preview of your color and blending-mode changes, choose Button on the Instance Behavior menu. Be sure to set the instance back to Movie Clip when you're finished.

- **Use the Free Transform tool.** You can transform instances of components, but not necessarily with the results you'd expect. Depending on the component, scaling an instance may change one dimension, both, or neither, and it doesn't affect text size at all. Skewing or rotating an instance works fine on the graphic part of the component, but it makes all text—labels and data—disappear. You can avoid this problem by embedding a font (see #99).

- **Edit the component.** Double-click an instance on the Stage to enter symbol editing mode, but with a difference: All the states of the component are shown (**Figure 97b**). Double-click one of the states to edit it as you would a standard symbol. (If you want a particular change to affect multiple states, you have to edit each one individually.) You can change the graphic portion (**Figure 97c**), but you can't change the appearance of the text—that can be done only through ActionScript. When you edit one instance of a component, the changes you make affect *all* instances of that component in your movie.

Tip

To change an edited component back to its original appearance, drag another copy of the component from the Components panel to the Library, then choose "Replace existing items."

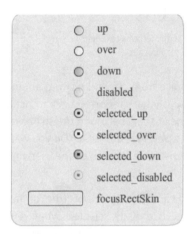

Figure 97b When you edit a component (in this case, the Radio Button), Flash shows you all of its possible states. To apply a change to multiple states, you must edit each individually.

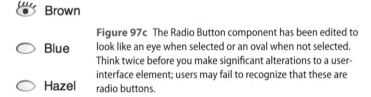

Figure 97c The Radio Button component has been edited to look like an eye when selected or an oval when not selected. Think twice before you make significant alterations to a user-interface element; users may fail to recognize that these are radio buttons.

- **Use ActionScript.** Although you can't use ActionScript to make radical changes in a component's appearance, you can change attributes such as its size and visibility. You can also make changes in the font, size, and style of the component's text. For an example of how Action-Script is used to set these parameters, see #98.

#98 Setting Parameters for Component Instances

You can think of the *properties* of a component instance as referring to outward characteristics such as size and color, and *parameters* as referring to more functional aspects. Each component has a different set of parameters, but here are some of the more common ones:

- **Label.** A *label* is the text that's associated with an instance.

- **Label Placement.** The standard placement of the label varies according to the component (**Figure 98a**).

Name [   ]   ☐ I agree   [SUBMIT]

Figure 98a A label is typically placed to the left of a text field, to the right of a check box, and directly on a button.

- **Value.** When a user makes a choice from a menu or from among a group of radio buttons, the *value* is what's reported back to ActionScript. The value is often the same as the label, but it doesn't have to be. For example, if a user chooses "Yes" in response to "Do you want a sales representative to call you?" the value (unseen by the user) might be "sucker."

- **Selected.** This parameter, which can have a value of "true" or "false," determines whether an instance is already selected when it first appears on the Stage—for example, whether a check box initially has a check in it.

- **Enabled.** Selecting "false" for the enabled parameter causes an instance to appear dimmed on the Stage.

- **Visible.** Selecting "false" for the visible parameter causes the instance to disappear from the Stage entirely.

There are three ways to set an instance's parameters:

- **Use the Parameters tab of the Property inspector.** When an instance of a component is selected on the Stage, clicking the Property inspector's Parameters tab shows you a table of the instance's primary parameters. A default value is filled in for each one, but you can change them. Some of the values are in editable text fields; others are on menus (**Figure 98b**).

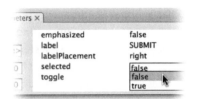

Figure 98b In the table shown here for the Button component, the value of the "label" parameter is editable text, while the value of the "selected" parameter is chosen from a menu.

- **Use the Component Inspector.** Open the Component Inspector panel by choosing Window > Component Inspector. The Parameters tab includes a table similar to the one in the Property inspector, but with more parameters. Changing a value here causes the same value to be changed in the Property inspector, and vice versa.

- **Use ActionScript.** To use this method to set parameters for a component instance, you must give it an instance name (see #90). The Action-Script code for setting parameters takes this general form:

```
instanceName.parameter = value
```

For this example, assume we have an instance of the CheckBox component called checkBox1. To change the instance's label and add a check mark, we could put the following code in a frame 1 script:

```
checkBox1.label="I use Flash";
checkBox1.selected=true;
```

Writing this script doesn't change anything in the authoring environment; it takes effect only when you test or publish the movie (**Figure 98c**).

Figure 98c On the left, the check box instance as it appears in the FLA file; on the right, the same instance as a SWF file in the Flash Player.

The simple syntax shown here is useful only for the parameters that are listed in the Component Inspector. Changing other characteristics of an instance requires more elaborate scripting, as you'll see in #99.

Help with Help

It's not easy to find out which parameters you can change with ActionScript and what the syntax is for changing them. Going to the Help panel and searching for keywords such as "components" and "parameters" doesn't get you very far. The best thing to do is choose ActionScript 3.0 Components from the menu at the upper left of the Help panel, then expand the ActionScript 3.0 Language and Components category, and within that, the All Classes category. You'll see a list of items such as "Check-Box class" and "RadioButton class." Click the class corresponding to the component you're using. All of its scriptable properties and styles (among other things) are displayed in the right pane. Also take a look at the UIComponent class, which includes properties shared by all the user-interface components.

#99 Formatting Text in a Component Label

Usually, the first thing you'll want to change about a component instance is the appearance of its label; the default font is small and unexciting.

Changing the label properties is tricky, because the label is a separate entity. In ActionScript terms, it's an instance of the TextFormat class inside an instance of the component. In this case, think of a *class* as being an abstract version of a symbol. The TextFormat class represents a generic, featureless hunk of text; we can create instances of that class with specific fonts, styles, and sizes.

Staying with the example we used in #98, assume we want the label for checkBox1 to be in 16-point Gill Sans italic. We start by creating a new instance of the TextFormat class, which we'll name niceText:

```
var niceText:TextFormat = new TextFormat();
```

We can then set the properties for that instance:

```
niceText.font="Gill Sans";
niceText.italic=true;
niceText.size=16;
```

Finally, we set the style for checkBox1. The specific style property we're setting is `textFormat`, and the model we're using is the instance we called niceText.

```
checkBox1.setStyle("textFormat", niceText);
```

The finished script is shown in **Figure 99a**; the published movie is shown in **Figure 99b**.

```
1   checkBox1.label="I use Flash";
2   checkBox1.selected=true;
3   var niceText:TextFormat = new TextFormat();
4   niceText.font="Gill Sans";
5   niceText.italic=true;
6   niceText.size=16;
7   checkBox1.setStyle("textFormat", niceText);
```

Figure 99a The finished script (including the two lines we wrote in #98) is displayed in the Actions panel.

Figure 99b The check box instance looks like this in the final movie. Compare the enhanced label to the default version in Figure 98c.

Using Components with ActionScript 3.0

You may choose to embed the font that's used in a label. This isn't required, but it's good insurance in case the user's computer doesn't have the font installed. It also keeps the label from disappearing if the component instance is rotated or skewed (see #97). The only drawback to embedding a font is that it increases the size of the SWF file.

To embed the Gill Sans font that's used in the label for checkBox1:

1. Create a new font symbol by right-clicking (Windows) or Control-clicking (Mac) inside the Library and choosing New Font from the contextual menu.

2. In the Font Symbol Properties dialog box, name the symbol gillSans (or whatever name you prefer) and choose its font, style, and size (**Figure 99c**). Click OK.

   The font symbol appears in the Library.

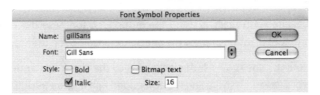

Figure 99c The Font Symbol Properties dialog box is set for 16-point Gill Sans italic.

3. Right-click (Windows) or Control-click (Mac) the font symbol and choose Linkage from the contextual menu.

4. In the Linkage Properties dialog box, select "Export for ActionScript." Flash fills in the "Class" field with the name of your font symbol. It also fills in the "Base class" field. The information in these fields allows ActionScript to recognize the font symbol.

5. Write down the name that Flash put into the Class field (in this case gillSans). Click OK.

   If an alert box appears, click OK again.

6. In the Actions panel, add the following line to the top of your frame 1 script:

   ```
   var embeddedFont:Font=new gillSans();
   ```

(continued on next page)

This creates an instance of the font symbol and gives it the name embeddedFont (or whatever you'd like to call it).

The word after "new" is the class name that you wrote down in the preceding step.

7. Go to the line in which you formerly specified a font for the niceText instance. Delete the font name and rewrite the line as follows:

```
niceText.font=embeddedFont.fontName;
```

(If you used a different instance name in step 6, use it instead of "embeddedFont.") The revised code tells niceText to use the embedded font rather than the one on the user's computer.

8. Add one more line to the end of the script, giving the check box instance permission to use the embedded font:

```
checkBox1.setStyle("embedFonts", true);
```

9. To make sure Flash really is using the embedded font, use the Free Transform tool to rotate or skew the checkBox1 instance on the Stage.

10. Test or publish the movie. If the label next to the check box appears rotated or skewed, Flash is using the embedded font (**Figure 99d**). If the text disappears, something went wrong—go through the steps again.

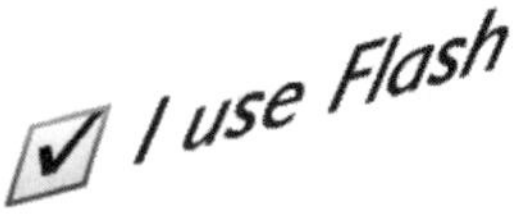

☑ *I use Flash*

Figure 99d Embedding a font allows a component's label to be rotated and/or skewed.

#100 Scripting User Interface Components

The component instances we've created in #97 through #99 look good, but they don't do anything useful. To make an instance respond to user input, you have to know the answer to two questions: First, what event do you want the instance to respond to—for example, a rollover, a mouse click, a key press? Second, what do you want to happen as a result?

Let's combine the check box that we've been working on with the happy/sad face movie that we made in #89 and refined in #90. What we want to happen is:

- When the check box is selected, the face becomes happy (**Figure 100a**).

- When the check box is deselected, the face becomes sad.

Figure 100a When the "I use Flash" check box is selected, the face becomes happy (left); when it's deselected, the face becomes sad (right).

Let's start by laying out the Timeline. It looks similar to **Figure 89b**, but the first frame has been deleted. There are now two segments: "happy" from frames 1 to 10 and "sad" from frames 11 to 20 (**Figure 100b**).

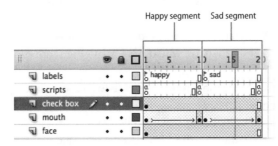

Figure 100b The Timeline has a happy segment and a sad segment, with a "stop" frame script at the end of each segment.

(continued on next page)

The instance of the check box component—which we'll call just "the check box" for short—is placed where the Happy and Sad buttons used to be, and it remains visible throughout the movie. In frame 1 of the scripts layer, we paste the script from **Figure 99a**. (For simplicity's sake, we're omitting the embedded font.)

If we were to test the movie at this point, the check box would function just as it did before. Independently, the face would start out neutral, become happy, and then stop.

Now let's tie the movement of the face to the events in the check box. When the movie begins, the check box is selected and the face becomes happy: That's exactly what we want to happen. When the user clicks the check box to deselect it, we want the face to turn sad. To make that happen, we can add the following function to the frame 1 script:

```
function mouseResponse(event:MouseEvent):void {
 if (currentFrame<11) {
        gotoAndPlay("sad");
  } else {
        gotoAndPlay("happy");
      }
}
```

The function here is named mouseResponse, but you can name it anything you like. When the user clicks the mouse, if the playhead is anywhere in the happy segment, it moves to the beginning of the sad segment; if it's anywhere in the sad segment, it moves to the beginning of the happy segment. (We cheated here and used a frame number instead of a frame label, but doing otherwise would have made the script too complicated.)

We want this function to be triggered in response to a mouse click in the check box. To accomplish this, we use an *event listener*—the capability of an object to sense when it's being clicked, rolled over, or otherwise interacted with and then to transmit the event to a defined function.

We add an event listener to the check box with a single line of ActionScript:

```
checkBox1.addEventListener(MouseEvent.CLICK, mouseResponse);
```

This code adds an event listener to checkBox1 that waits for a click of the mouse. When it detects one, it activates the mouseResponse function.

Using Components with ActionScript 3.0

The finished script (**Figure 100c**) produces the results that were shown in **Figure 100a**. It doesn't do so in the most polished or foolproof way—for example, the script doesn't know whether the check box is selected at any given time—but it should be simple and clear enough to get you started with writing your own scripts.

```
1   checkBox1.label="I use Flash";
2   checkBox1.selected=true;
3   var niceText:TextFormat = new TextFormat();
4   niceText.font="Gill Sans";
5   niceText.italic=true;
6   niceText.size=16;
7   checkBox1.setStyle("textFormat", niceText);
8   function mouseResponse(event:MouseEvent):void {
9       if (currentFrame<11) {
10          gotoAndPlay("sad");
11      } else {
12          gotoAndPlay("happy");
13      }
14  }
15  checkBox1.addEventListener(MouseEvent.CLICK, mouseResponse);
16
```

Figure 100c The finished script contains an event listener and a function that's triggered when the event occurs.

Index

Index

Index

Index

Index

Index

Index

Index

Index

Index

Index

Index

Index

Index

W

WAV format, 142
waveforms, 142, 150, 154
Web browsers
  alternative content, 190
  animated GIFs in, 178
  Internet Explorer, 188
  opening pages in, 12
  playing movies in, 144,
    180–181
  playing SWF files in,
    16, 84
  window size, 184
Web pages
  displaying movies in,
    180–181
  QuickTime files in, 193
Web search engines, 10
web servers, 162
white
  blending modes, 116
  as starting color, 26
Window Mode menu, 185

windows
  floating, 7
  workspace, 8
Windows Media (WMV)
  format, 158, 160
Windows systems
  DirectX, 160
  Movie Maker, 160
  projectors, 179, 192
  Windows Media and,
    158
WMV (Windows Media)
  format, 158, 160
workspaces
  adding color to, 24
  adding symbols to, 53
  arranging, 4–9
  Bridge, 122
  configuring, 8–9
  default, 8
  described, 8
  saved, 8